Sally Alter, R.N.

HOW TO LIVE WITH BIPOLAR

**Bipolar Basics • Coping with Bipolar • Depression
Mania • Psychosis • Anxiety • Relationships**

Published by: Amazon

Sally Alter https://wirsinddu.eu/sally_alter

Cover design & formatting: Rew Mitchell, rewkachu.com
Cover design: David A. Feingold, D.E.d., LCSW

For Hal Robinson

who helped me find myself

and

Kathleen Pennell

whose unwavering encouragement

helped me write this book.

CONTENTS

INTRODUCTION

In 1972, when I lived in London, I found a paperback book at a used book shop called "*Mood Swings.*" I don't remember the name of the author. Since I had already experienced ten years of mood swings by that time, it made very interesting reading.

The book explained many things I did not know. It also noted that some people find they have latent bipolar disorder when they have a manic or hypomanic episode on taking anti-depressants for depression.

This was exactly what had happened to me, over and over again, since I was fifteen. I would get very depressed, take anti-depressants, and end up having a mood swing into mania.

Armed with this new knowledge, I went to see my doctor and showed him my rather tattered paperback. The doctor prescribed a course of Lithium which worked very well for twenty-two years, except I developed hypothyroidism from the Lithium which is not uncommon.

I have since suffered from bipolar 1 disorder with psychotic tendencies all my life. During that time, I have spent fourteen months in various hospitals and had more changes of medication than I can count.

Fortunately, I have found the right combination of medicines now, and have not had any further mood swings.

For the past two and a half years, I have been writing about bipolar disorder on Quora, an international question and answer website. During that time, I have been the *Most Viewed Writer* every month, have answered 800 questions on bipolar and mental health, and have 13 million views to date. I am also an R.N. and have studied bipolar disorder and mental illness for many years.

This is not a text book and I am not a doctor. The questions and answers in this book are taken from some of my answers on Quora. They are real questions with real answers. The people who ask these questions need help managing their bipolar illness.

When it comes to bipolar, knowledge is power, and I am happy to share my experiences and my research with you, my readers. I hope you will be able to relate to many of the questions and answers in this book.

WHAT IS BIPOLAR DISORDER?

Bipolar disorder (previously called manic depression) is a severe mood disorder that adversely effects a person's everyday activities.

Most people have varying moods as part of living. They may feel down for a couple of days when things go wrong, and they may well refer to that as depression. But even though they feel depressed, their mood is nothing compared to the depression felt by a person with bipolar.

Bipolar depression is more severe and disabling. It also lasts for an extended period of time and results in a loss of functioning.

A person with bipolar depression will feel lethargic. They will talk and move slowly because they have little energy. They will feel sad, guilty and worthless. They may want to isolate away from their relatives and friends. With depression comes a total loss of motivation, even for things once enjoyed. All the person wants to do is lie down on the couch and go to sleep.

If the depression continues to get worse, they will lose interest in everything around them and take to their bed. They will have no energy to shower or even brush their teeth. When depression becomes severe the person needs emergency care.

Similarly, when someone says they are manic because they have had a few days of feeling happy, that is not bipolar mania as they would feel ecstatic or irritable far beyond the normal everyday mood. They would need very little sleep (4 to 5 hours a night) yet not feel tired and have an enormous amount of energy.

Bipolar mania is the opposite of depression. The person suddenly finds he has a lot to do and no time to do it. He may well take on various projects, be far more talkative than usual, indulge in risky behavior and abuse various substances.

When bipolar mania or depression become severe their mood can escalate to psychosis causing the person to hallucinate and experience delusions.

There is much publicity surrounding bipolar disorder these days, and people think it is more prevalent than it is. According to documented sources it effects approximately 5.7m adults and 2.8% of the population in America and 45m people around the world. There is still a great deal of stigma attached to bipolar disorder, and indeed to all mental illnesses.

There are four recognized types of bipolar disorder:

1. **Bipolar 1**
2. **Bipolar 2**
3. **Cyclothymia**
4. **Bipolar NOS** (not otherwise specified)

We will discuss bipolar 1 and bipolar 2 for the purposes of this book.

PART ONE
Bipolar basics

How do I know if I have bipolar?

Bipolar disorder usually begins in late adolescence, or early twenties, so it is sometimes difficult to know if it is actually the illness talking or hormonal changes taking place in the body.

Many people are emotionally unstable and have natural mood swings. They may be going through a difficult period in their lives where they are under a lot of stress. Or they may have read too much about the illness and are afraid that they might have it. Fortunately, their symptoms are not always bipolar.

In fact, bipolar is a relatively rare disorder affecting less than 3% of the population.

Even today, there is still a lot of stigma surrounding the illness, so if you make your own diagnosis, you can condemn yourself to a life-time of misery. That's why you have to leave it up to a health professional to make a correct diagnosis and prescribe suitable treatment.

Bipolar usually begins with a manic or depressive episode which comes on out of the blue. Some sources say that boys/men often experience a manic episode first, whereas it is more common for girls/women to present with signs of depression at the start of the illness.

Even when a person has a manic/hypomanic episode it may not be recognized as bipolar, and those episodes are often later forgotten making diagnosis difficult. People do not generally go to see a doctor if they are in mania/hypomania because they generally feel well and happy.

The reverse is true of depression. Many people go to see their doctor because they have a depressive mood that will not lift. But as previous manic/hypomanic episodes are often forgotten when taking a history, it Is hard to diagnose their mood swings as being related to bipolar.

An average diagnosis from a mental health professional takes 10 years from the onset of the illness.

Are there any laboratory tests for bipolar disorder?

No, there are no laboratory tests, x-rays, MRIs, CAT scans, or anything else to determine if someone has bipolar disorder at this point in time. The diagnosis is made by a qualified medical professional based on the following:

A thorough physical examination.

Extensive history-taking.

Strict criteria as laid out in the DSM V.
(*Diagnostic & Statistical Manual of Mental Disorders 5th edition*).

- For Bipolar 1, a person has to have had at least one manic episode lasting a week, or necessitating a hospital stay. Depressive episodes are not necessary for this diagnosis.
- Bipolar 2 is diagnosed if a person has had at least one hypo-manic episode and major depressive episodes.

Patients are notoriously bad at giving a detailed history of their symptoms. This is one of the reasons why it takes ten years, on average, before a diagnosis of bipolar disorder is made. People will often go to see a doctor when they are depressed, but rarely when they are manic or hypomanic because they don't think they are ill. All they can remember is having felt euphoric or very irritable at some time in the past but not the details as mania tricks you into thinking nothing is wrong with you.

If a faulty diagnosis of major depressive disorder is given, the patient will more than likely be treated with anti-depressants. This can sometimes cause a rebound effect of mania or hypomania, especially with SSRIs, which can then give a more accurate diagnosis of bipolar disorder.

If you are going to see a doctor for a diagnosis, it is best to think back on all your symptoms and write them down before your appointment. You might ask those closest to you for their opinion as this may well differ from yours. This will help the psychiatrist enormously, and get you the correct diagnosis and treatment in a timely fashion.

What are the risks of undiagnosed bipolar?

The risks are great when it comes to bipolar disorder. Unlike many other mental illnesses, bipolar is a potentially fatal disease. The risk of suicide is so high that 13% to 22% of people with bipolar will die by their own hands, and another 50% will make at least one attempt at suicide in their lifetime.

Even without the threat of suicide, bipolar is a very destructive disorder and many lives have been left in ruins when the illness has been allowed to run wild and out of control.

Also, bipolar is often accompanied by self-destructive behaviors like alcohol and street drug abuse. This is called dual diagnosis. Bipolar is so hard to live with that people often resort to self-medication.

Depression can cause untold misery in people's lives. Feeling tired all the time, and unable to think clearly, makes it very difficult to succeed in life. People fail at school due to depression, and many people are not able to work at all.

Mania is often worse if left untreated. When manic, people make impulsive decisions that are responsible for many bankruptcies, accidents, job losses, divorces, financial hardships and impulsive sexual affairs. Not to mention the relationships with friends and family that are ruined by the person's manic behavior.

Years can be wasted to bipolar disorder. People who are not adequately medicated will no doubt have great difficulty achieving anything in life because of the relentless mood swings. Bipolar is a severe mental illness and needs managing with medication and therapy if possible.

What does undiagnosed bipolar 1 look like?
How does diagnosing help?

Bipolar disorder is classed as a severe mental illness. Bipolar 1 is the worst form of the illness on the bipolar spectrum. People who have bipolar 1 suffer with mania which is a more serious form of hypomania (experienced by people with bipolar 2). When the illness is badly controlled, the person has to be admitted to the hospital. So, as you can see, it is very unlikely that a person with this severe illness hasn't seen a doctor in the past.

A person with bipolar 1 (like a person with bipolar 2) may have very severe depressions which do not resemble the normal bad moods that everybody experiences in life. They do not feel fed up and bored for a few days like most people do at times, their symptoms are very exaggerated when in a depressive episode.

Depression in bipolar 1 (and in bipolar 2) includes the following symptoms:

- Feeling sad, guilty and worthless.

- Feeling very irritable or angry.

- Drastic loss of energy.

- Eating disturbances.

- Loss of motivation, even for things a person once enjoyed.

- Tendency to isolate and avoid contact with other people.

- Persistent thoughts of death and suicide.

It is worth noting, that bipolar 1 can be diagnosed without a history of depressive episodes.

When a person is in mania, they feel euphoric and experience a great surge of energy. This is the opposite of the loss of energy felt in a depressive cycle. They do not feel tired and feel that sleeping is a waste of time. They may only sleep for four to five hours a night and still feel energetic in the morning.

Mania in bipolar1 includes the following symptoms:

- Feelings of omnipotence and superiority.
- Thinking and speaking fast.
- Feelings of anger and rage.
- Enormous surge of energy.
- Sleep disturbances.
- Rapid speech and thought processes.
- Starting new projects but never finishing them.

When manic, a person usually takes enormous risks like driving too fast, drinking too much, gambling all their money away, making risky business decisions, over-shopping, having promiscuous encounters that can result in pregnancy, or break up of previous relationships.

A person with bipolar 1 can also be subject to psychosis if the symptoms of depression or mania are severe. Psychosis is being unable to distinguish what is real and what is false.

Psychosis in bipolar 1 includes the following symptoms:

- Loss of touch with reality.
- Sleep and eating changes.
- Hallucinations, delusions and/or paranoia.
- Feelings of anger or violence.
- Agitation and irritation.

It is very difficult to live with this illness. People often have many hospital admissions throughout their lives. When a person has a correct diagnosis the usual course of treatment is medication (in particular, mood-stabilizers) and therapy.

There is no cure for bipolar 1 disorder (or any illness on the bipolar spectrum). It is a lifelong condition. Medication must be taken every day for life. Therapy is recommended to heal past traumas and help the person cope with everyday problems that will arise with this illness.

Bipolar 1 is a very complex illness, not easily understood by most people. If you are given this diagnosis by a doctor, it is wise to study the illness as much as you can and do your best to find a good support system to help you during the bad episodes.

How often are symptoms of bipolar disorder mistaken for depression?

This happens quite often. As you know, bipolar has two poles, one being depression, the other being mania or hypomania. When a person is depressed with bipolar their symptoms are the same as in clinical depression.

Some people would say that depression in major depressive disorder is worse than in bipolar, and the depressions lasts for a longer duration. But it is really impossible to know for sure as nobody can experience both illness at the same time unless they are unfortunate enough to have a dual diagnosis.

A person who is depressed will feel very sad and guilty. In many cases they will also feel hopeless and worthless as a person. When depressed a person has no energy or motivation to do anything. Since depression is the same in both mood disorders it is sometimes difficult to differentiate one from another.

However, it must be noted that the longer the depression goes on the more chance there is of suicidal behavior, either attempts or completion of the act. It is very important when you are depressed to try to communicate these feelings to others as they can be helpful. If not, there is always the *National Suicide Hotline*. You can call them even if you are not suicidal because they are there to listen to what people have to share. Their phone number is below.

Many people with depression are treated initially with anti-depressants. If they have a manic reaction, the diagnosis is then changed to bipolar. Anti-depressants are generally ill-advised for bipolar patients, especially the SSRIs, because they have been known to cause problems.

Bipolar is very hard to diagnose. It takes an expert clinician to understand the difference between bipolar and depression. They need to take a really thorough history from the person to be sure of the diagnosis.

Hopefully, this will make the person remember something they may have dismissed at the time as being just a good mood. If nobody brought it to their attention that they were acting out of character at the time, they are very likely to have forgotten it. It takes on average ten years to diagnose bipolar.

National Suicide Prevention Lifeline: 1 800 273-8255

I suffer from bipolar disorder and I'm trying to come off my mood stabilizer. How do I do it?

The standard treatment for bipolar disorder is mood-stabilizers. Other medications may be added to these for things like anxiety, psychosis, ADHD, and extreme depressive episodes, but as the name Implies, mood stabilizers help level out your moods and keep you stable.

You will find that every time you try to come off mood stabilizers you will be very ill. It makes perfectly good sense, when you think about it.

There are no two ways around it. Bipolar is a life long illness. There is no known cure, and it doesn't go away because you stop taking the medication.

If you want to stay well, you will need to keep taking the medications. That's the way it is with any chronic illness. It's the same with diabetes, high blood pressure, heart disease and hundreds of other conditions which have no cure. People have to take medications for the rest of their lives.

We need to be thankful there are medications that can help keep us well with this relentless disease.

For those with bipolar, what is worse mania or depression?

That is a very interesting question, and it forces me to assess my own situation. Over all, I would say I definitely find depression worse. I have bipolar and when depressed I just want to die. Nobody and nothing can change my way of thinking about that. I am in such pain. I just want it to stop.

People say, "You will feel better tomorrow", and they are possibly right, but it is not something I want to hear when I am depressed because I don't believe it. Depression causes your mind to act illogically. You cannot see reason at all. People may care, but don't understand.

I think about mania in a thoroughly different way. I have had so many dreadful incidents that I could put down to mania (if not, what?) that I would have forgotten if you hadn't reminded me now.

I can't count the number of times I have reacted to things that were none of my business. I have said and done many things I would happily take back if I could. Most of these things took place in church and must have proved to the congregation, over and over again, that indeed I was mentally ill. The vast majority of people just ignored me - others looked on with mock-sympathy.

However, other things I have thought about don't fall into the category of mania, or even hypo-mania because they don't last long enough. This makes me certain that bipolar 1 is not managed completely by medication. Even with the best medicine in the world, bipolar has a nasty habit of breaking through the barrier that is blocking true mania or hypomania.

You can have many episodes of depression and mania, but in between these episodes you may still experience what I call blips. My blips may only last a day, or even an hour, but they are self-deprecating and cause terrible destruction.

I have misinterpreted many situations, spoken out angrily about things that I have not understood in one of my manic blips. I could name dozens of incidents, but I am too embarrassed to think of them now. I will tell you one of these blips. It is not one of my worst, but really strange anyhow.

Once a couple in church had part of their house burn down. They were needing somewhere to stay while the repair work was being done. Now a 'normal' (not bipolar) person would have realized that they couldn't help and said nothing, but that did not occur to me. In my confusion, I burst into tears. Then, with tears flowing down my face, I rushed up to the couple and offered my house to them.

I said I only had one bed but they could use it and I would sleep on the couch. It never occurred to me that the repairs to their house might take months and I would get tired of sleeping on the couch. It is not possible to think straight when snatched up in the whirlwind of bipolar.

Are bipoplar and personality two separate things?

The difference, as I see it, is when you have a physical illness your personality remains the same. Not so in bipolar.

Many people like to compare bipolar to diabetes, but this is mainly due to the fact that they need medication or insulin every day to remain well (and indeed to live) but their personality does not change just because they are ill. If they were a happy person, or a miserable person before their illness they will generally remain that way after a diagnosis.

It is not that way with bipolar disorder. When you have mood swings it does indeed appear that your personality has changed, and you could say that it had for the length of time that you are in that particular mood. It is very difficult, if not impossible, to be a happy person when you are depressed. And, likewise, when you are manic or hypo-manic, it changes you to a very exuberant or irritable person. Many people find this very confusing indeed.

It is possible to consider bipolar as having three moods and not just two. There is the depressive mood, the manic/hypomanic mood and the euthymic mood which is when you are well. The real you.

However, you must always remember that you are still the same person underneath the mood swings. I like to say there is Sally and there is Sally's illness. We are not one and the same. I am still my own person just because I have an illness. That is why I object to people saying you are bipolar. I am not bipolar; I just have an illness called bipolar.

The problem is that when you are in the throes of depression it is very hard to remember that you are not always like that. It is in fact hard to hang on to the person you used to be. And the same goes for mania and hypo-mania. You definitely exhibit different personality traits during those mood swings. It is hard to maintain just one personality when you have bipolar.

How can I help myself? I have bipolar and feel like ending it all.

I am sorry to hear that you feel so desperate. Having been suicidal many times myself, I know that thinking about death and dying all the time is really distressing.

The best way to help yourself is to take a look at the symptoms of bipolar depression and realize that these thoughts are quite normal:

- Feelings of sadness, guilt, worthlessness and hopelessness.

- No motivation to do anything, even the things you once enjoyed.

- Exhaustion most of the time.

- Sleeping either too much or too little.

- Eating either too much or too little.

- Neglecting personal hygiene.

- Thoughts of death and suicide.

It is difficult to see these feelings of death and dying as symptoms because they seem so real, but that is what they are. Make a list of all the things you can do to distract yourself when they occur then they won't take on such importance.

The main thing is not to act upon your feelings. Thinking about suicide is one thing, but making a plan is quite another. If it would put your mind at rest, be sure to put all medications, knives and guns out of sight. Or get somebody responsible to do this for you.

If these symptoms persist, and you start making plans to carry them out, please call the *National Suicide Hot Line*. Even if you don't feel like carrying out your plans at that moment, you may get some relief by talking your problems over with somebody else. They have online chat if you don't want to speak to a live person.

Bipolar Disorder has a high risk of suicide and you don't want to become a casualty of this illness.

Suicide is a permanent solution to a temporary problem.

National Suicide Prevention Lifeline: 1 800 273-8255

Does bipolar cause physical symptoms?

Although bipolar is a mood disorder, it can have a significant impact on a person's physical state. One thing that is always affected is the energy level. Bipolar is an illness that drains a person's energy in the depressive phase and increases it in the manic phase.

It also affects the person's sleep cycle. Many people in a depressive phase sleep for 12–16 hours a day (hypersomnia), and some may not be able to get to sleep, or wake up during the night (insomnia). It is not uncommon to be so fatigued that a person doesn't have the energy (or the inclination) to get out of bed. Showering, or even brushing one's teeth, becomes a monumental task.

When in depression, many people have flu-like aches and pains, and feel heavy with sore muscles. Irritability, that often comes with depression or mania, can be accompanied by nausea, vomiting or diarrhea.

People in a manic phase usually experience sleep disturbance. That is often the first symptom of mania. People can operate quite successfully on only three to five hours sleep a night. Some people never feel tired at all and think that sleeping is a waste of time because they have too many things to do. People in mania are sometimes up during the night sorting out cupboards, doing housework, even scrubbing the grout in the kitchen tiles with a toothbrush!

Appetite is often affected by bipolar disorder, either by eating too much or too little. Also, many bipolar medications cause quite considerable weight gain. This can be very upsetting and must be discussed with the prescribing doctor. Agreement is usually reached when deciding on the pros and cons to a person's health.

Sexual performance can also be affected; loss of libido in depression and having a very high libido in mania (hypersexuality). This can cause many problems in the various phases of bipolar disorder. Medication, especially SSRI anti-depressants, can be the culprit in causing problems with sexual performance.

Heart rate can also be affected, increasing considerably in mania. The blood pressure can produce higher readings, as well. In anxiety or panic attacks, which often accompany bipolar, the person can have hyperventilation events which are very disturbing. Panic also causes trouble with breathing and sweaty palms, but this is not permanent. Also, many people have dual-diagnoses in bipolar as they sometimes drink too much or take street drugs to cope with the everyday ups and downs of the illness.

There are sometimes long-term serious side effects from bipolar medication (like kidney disease, hypothyroid, and high blood pressure from Lithium).

The average reduction in life expectancy in people with bipolar is between 9 and 20 years. This is often due to the high suicide rate of 50% of attempted suicides and 13% - 22% of completed acts.

I've tried running from my bipolar diagnosis but I keep getting sick. What should I do?

It is really hard to accept a diagnosis of bipolar. It is very tempting to deny it and want to run away from it. But you can't run far because bipolar disorder never leaves you. It is like the unwelcome guest at the party. You may think you can get rid of him, but he just won't go.

Some people are lucky and have episodes months or even years apart. But even if your episodes are rare, you can never let your guard down. Once you have bipolar, you will always have bipolar. You may think it has gone away but it will come back to bite you in the end. Bipolar is a lifelong illness.

There is a lot of stigma attached to this illness, or rather to all mental illnesses, and it is sometimes difficult to get past the "Why me?" stage. But of course, "Why not me?" Why should I be any different from other people? The important thing is to avoid the Victim. We all have a Victim inside us when it comes to bipolar, but it does no good complaining. We had best accept it and learn to live with it.

I have had bipolar for many years. I won't tell you how many years it took me to accept my diagnosis because I would curl up and die with embarrassment. I thought, "Surely this doesn't apply to me. It can't be true." I even remember going to see my psychiatrist at the local mental health clinic one day and asking him, "Do I have a mental illness?" He stared at me over his bifocals and frowned.

I had been going to that clinic for years, had taken about twenty different cocktails of medication, even been in hospital many times over, yet still I didn't want to admit that I could have such a damaging diagnosis as bipolar disorder. So, I really understand where you are coming from I really do.

Unfortunately, there is as yet no cure for bipolar. Although it has no cure it can be managed with medication, therapy and life style changes. Be sure to take good care of yourself to remain well.

Take your medications regularly as prescribed. This is your main defense against symptoms. Therapy usually goes along with bipolar treatment, so if you can afford it find a suitable professional who can help you with your everyday problems. Many people find Cognitive Behavioral Therapy (CBT) helpful in changing your negative thinking patterns.

It is also wise to think carefully about your lifestyle and to make changes where needed. Go to bed and get up at the same time every day. Eat a proper diet and get out in the sunshine whenever you can. Exercise is also good for bipolar, especially in the depressive phase when you don't feel like doing anything. Just ten minutes walking round the block is better than doing nothing. It really pays to help yourself when you have this illness.

What works for bipolar alongside getting on the right medication?

The three pillars of treatment for bipolar disorder are:

1. **Medication**
2. **Therapy**
3. **Lifestyle**

It is like a three-legged stool. If one or two of the legs are missing, it can be very difficult to balance. And if nothing else, bipolar is a balancing act. In order to be successful, you need to get as much balance in your life as possible.

Medication

There is no doubt that medication is the first line of defense against bipolar disorder. It is important to get it right, but it is also important to be patient for medication to work. Many medications have side effects, and some can be dangerous, so you may have to try a number of 'medication cocktails' before you find one that suits you.

If you think about it carefully, you will realize what a very small part it plays in your life. I am only guessing at these figures as everybody's situation is different, but let's say it takes you:

- One hour to see a psychiatrist once a month.
- Half an hour to get the prescription filled.
- Half an hour to actually swallow the pills.

If all goes well, you have spent two hours a month on medically treating your bipolar illness!

That's great! The question then is "What do you do with the rest of the time to stay well?"

Therapy

Bipolar disorder is so destructive to your everyday life that therapy in one form or another is (almost) essential. It is important to discuss with your prospective therapist what type of therapy they provide as it is not a one size fits all situation with bipolar. Many people do well with Cognitive Behavioral Therapy (CBT) as this helps regulate the negative thoughts of bipolar disorder. Others prefer another form of therapy entirely. And there are many different therapies out there.

So now you have spent maybe another four hours in therapy a month.

That still leaves you a great deal of time to work on staying well. Many people say that bipolar is a full-time job!

Lifestyle

The sad fact is that with a diagnosis of bipolar disorder you will probably not be able to do all the things you used to do and hope to stay well.

- Work on your bedtime routine as sleep plays a major part in keeping well. It is no longer wise to go out with your friends and drink and party until 3 in the morning. You need to go to bed at the same time each night and wake up at the same time each morning. This is the essence of good sleep hygiene.

- You also need to take a look at your diet. No more bars of chocolate for lunch, or packets of chips for dinner, you now have to take care of what you put into your body to stay well.

- Exercise is another thing that is necessary when you have bipolar. Try to do half an hour a day and that will help your mood enormously. Endorphins are produced when you exercise and go a long way to helping with depression.

These are the basic three approaches to staying well, but study more about bipolar on line and you will see that there are many other things you can fit into your daily routine.

With this new lifestyle you have a far greater chance of success than just popping a pill and hoping it will do all the work. You need to take responsibility for yourself in order to stay well with bipolar.

I have bipolar 2 and am on lots of meds. It makes me really upset. How can i cope?

Bipolar is a very difficult illness to live with. I really empathize with you as I have bipolar myself. Many people think they know all about bipolar but it is a very complex illness and not easy to understand. People understand depression, to a certain extent, but bipolar is far more complicated with added mood swings like hypomania and mania. People with bipolar 2 only have hypomania, not full-blown mania, but that is no fun.

You may need to study it more to find out what you can expect when living with this disorder. There are many books, articles and magazines devoted to the subject. And plenty of autobiographies, so you can see how other people have coped. It is always good to keep up to date with your studies as knowledge of this illness is changing all the time. Also, there are new treatments coming on the market, and you need to be interested in the medications you are taking. It is important that you look out for any side-effects when starting on a new medication.

Many people, maybe like you, start to feel better when they are on the right medication. They begin to think the illness must have gone away so they stop taking the medication. Unfortunately, bipolar does not go away. The only reason they felt better is because the medication was working.

I know it is very hard to accept you have this disorder as there is still so much stigma attached to it. I had tremendous problems with denial myself. But eventually it pays to come to terms with it and do all you can to stay well.

Yes, it is annoying to have to take so many medications, but with a lifelong illness like bipolar it is necessary to take them every day to stop the mood swings. If you have to take a little pill or two to stay well, I think you will find it is far better than having to put up with mood swings.

It is also important that you take responsibility for the illness. Medication will definitely help, it is the first line of defense, but you will need to do other things yourself.

Decide to change your lifestyle to stay well and you won't regret it. Make sure you get enough sleep, go to bed and wake up at the same time every day if possible. Also, remember to eat regular, nutritious meals that will help your immune system. If you can do some exercise that will also help, especially if you are depressed as it raises the endorphins and gives you some needed energy.

Try to rest during the day by doing some relaxation exercises or creative visualization. There are many of these relaxation exercises on *YouTube*. Don't forget to play when you can, too. Think of all the things you love to do when you have the time and do them regularly. You may like gardening, cooking or painting. When you have Bipolar it is important to have fun.

Can bipolar go into remission without medication?

It can certainly fool you into thinking it could. However, bipolar is a cyclical illness. You can be sure it will cycle back when you are unaware. You may go for months, even years, without an episode, but don't you worry, it will come back sooner or later because you have bipolar disorder.

Bipolar is a severe form of mental illness, like schizophrenia. It is a life long illness because there is no cure. It can be managed, but even that is not always possible. To think you can do without medication is asking for trouble.

I have hypertension (as well as bipolar and many other chronic diseases) and take medication every day. What would happen if I decided I didn't want to take my medication anymore? It would be nice; I take too many medications as it is. But, at the end of the day, if I don't take my medication, I could have a stroke and die.

It is the same with a severe mental illness like bipolar. You need medication in order to stay alive and well. This illness has a very high suicidal rate. According to various sources 13 - 22% of people do actually kill themselves. 50% make attempts.

Why do they kill themselves? That is debatable, but if you have ever had bipolar depression for any length of time you will probably have been there and know for yourself. There is no end of problems with bipolar.

What happens when you go off your mood stabilizers is that you have what is affectionately called a 'med holiday' while the effects of the medication stay in your system. Then suddenly, without warning, the holiday comes to an end and you are either in hospital, or having to take higher doses of your medication - or both. It is just not worth the risk.

Mood stabilizers are just that. They stabilize your mood. If you want to be totally unbalanced, stopping your mood stabilizer is the way to go. I prefer to maintain a modicum of balance by taking my medication, and so should you.

How does a bipolar phase begin?

Bipolar varies so much from person to person it is difficult, if not impossible, to generalize. Some people find that episodes (phases) materialize slowly over a period of a week or so, but others just wake up one day and feel sick.

The episodes differ in bipolar 1 and bipolar 2 which adds to the confusion.

I gather you are referring to episodes of depression and hypomania/mania. This makes a marked difference as well. Depression is usually easy to recognize in oneself as you feel sad and lose your motivation to do anything, but hypomania/mania can be very sneaky and sometimes it is not possible to recognize that you are having an episode at all.

Personally, I like to be one step ahead of the game if I can by keeping a mood chart every day. This helps me notice when things are getting out of hand, and I also note any triggers which may cause an episode.

You can print out any number of online mood charts, or you can make your own. I tend to make my own as I don't need half the information they recommend, and often need to add things like rage or panic attacks.

There is also a wonderful program called *WRAP (Wellness Recovery Action Plan)* by Mary Ellen Copeland which you might find useful. WRAP is a way of monitoring yourself and your triggers. It also shows you how to prevent episodes from happening or getting worse.

WRAP has been taught at workshops Internationally for many years, and I would recommend finding out if there are any of these workshops in your area. If not, you can find a great deal of information online, as well as many books and workbooks on the subject.

How many pills do people usually take with bipolar?

This varies a great deal because bipolar disorder is a very difficult illness to treat. One psychiatrist might only prescribe a couple of medications to help control the symptoms whereas another psychiatrist might prescribe five.

People are all different. What is great for controlling symptoms for one person may not work at all for another. That is why it is never advisable to take another person's medication - it is also against the Law!

It is the general consensus of opinion that mood-stabilizers are the drug of choice for people with bipolar disorder. This does not mean a person can take a mood-stabilizer and always remain well. Sometimes other drugs like anti-depressants or anti-psychotics are needed to keep the person stable.

At various times in our lives we need different treatment, especially with bipolar. I remember going through menopause at forty-seven and my trusty Lithium, that had worked fine for the previous twenty-two years, suddenly stopped working and I became very sick. I tried about twenty-five different combinations of medications over the next few years until I finally got it right. That is why it pays to be patient. Don't think the first drug you take will work for you.

All medications have side effects, even aspirin, so you need to watch out for these, especially when you begin taking a new medication. Ask your doctor about the side effects when he is prescribing a new medication. Then go home and study them online.

Some side effects can be very serious, and the person will not be able to tolerate the drug at all. Drugs like anti-psychotics are prone to weight gain - sometimes 50 lbs. in the first three months. The psychiatrist and the patient will need to decide whether it is worth suffering some weight gain in order to stay well. Bipolar is such a devastating illness that many people decide to take the medication and try to adhere to a strict diet. It is not easy, but that is the price you pay for wellness.

Psychiatrists have various levels of expertise, and patients have various levels of resistance to medications, so you can never generalize when it comes to treating bipolar. Unfortunately, some people get no relief from medications at all as they are totally medication resistant. In those cases, they have to rely on therapy and lifestyle changes to stay well.

I have been tracking my moods for months and think I have bipolar. Will I be sent to a facility or to a psychiatrist?

First of all, congratulations for being smart enough to track your moods for such a long time. Many people who do actually have bipolar never get around to doing mood charts, and it is so helpful for you and your doctor to see what is happening in your everyday life.

Normally, when you go to a doctor, you can only think of what is happening today and not what lead up to it. That's why it is a good idea to be able to see patterns in your thinking and behavior. If you do the mood charts correctly, you may be able to see a trend. This will give you a heads up that a new mood swing is to follow.

You must have gained a lot of insight yourself from tracking your moods, but the danger in that is you may be misinterpreting them, and they are not indicative of bipolar disorder at all. Then you will have been worrying for nothing. Bipolar is still a fairly rare disorder affecting only 2.8% of the population.

The best way to check on this is to have a talk with your doctor and see what he thinks. There are strict criteria for bipolar disorder and you may not fit it at all.

Don't be afraid that you will be sent to a hospital. That would only happen if you were in a crisis situation and were a danger to yourself or others. If you were frankly suicidal, and had a plan to carry it out, then I think your doctor would send you to a hospital for your own safety. Psychiatric hospitals are usually full, so there is no way you would be sent to one if you are able to cope with your everyday life.

If your doctor does think you may have Bipolar, he will almost certainly refer you to a psychiatrist who will be able to help you with a true diagnosis and a treatment plan to make you feel better.

What's the difference between bipolar and schizophrenia?

I was always interested in this question myself and had a fear of having a schizophrenic diagnosis. It is bad enough having a diagnosis of bipolar let alone being diagnosed with schizophrenia. Stigma is alive and well in both illnesses, but I think it is worse in schizophrenia. Interestingly, doctors in different countries sometimes diagnose the same patient with either bipolar or schizophrenia. It can be very confusing.

There are a number of arguments on this subject. Some people are of the view that bipolar and schizophrenia are very alike, while others see a deep divide. There are certainly some things that appear to be similar, but when examined properly it can be seen that the illnesses are not one and the same.

Many people think that schizophrenia is devastating because it is unrelenting and causes untold suffering. Whereas bipolar, although a severe mental illness does have respite from mood swings, in most cases, and is not subject to frequent or lengthy psychotic episodes.

The major difference is that bipolar is a mood disorder whereas schizophrenia is a psychotic disorder.

People with bipolar suffer disruptive mood swings and people with schizophrenia suffer from hallucinations, delusions and problems in cognition much of the time although this can be controlled to a certain extent with medication.

When you are psychotic for long periods of time, as in schizophrenia, it is not possible to understand what is happening around you because you are unable to think clearly. You cannot concentrate or focus on anything and have difficulty understanding what other people are saying. Hallucinations and delusions seem real and your beliefs cannot be shaken. You are basically unable to distinguish fact from fiction.

Bipolar is like schizophrenia in as much as they both have psychotic episodes; however, it is usually only bipolar 1 that has psychosis and not bipolar 2. The psychoses in bipolar 1 sometimes occur with severe mania or severe depressive episodes. The symptoms are similar to those experienced by people with schizophrenia. Some say people with schizophrenia are more prone to hearing voices than people with bipolar, but there is nothing to say one is worse than the other. Psychosis is terrible no matter who has it.

Schizophrenia is diagnosed as an illness with psychotic symptoms like hallucinations, delusions and paranoia. It naturally follows that people with this illness suffer more from psychosis. Bipolar psychoses are generally much shorter, and in between episodes people can usually live a relatively normal life.

Are there any mental disorders that can cause mania but not depression?

Yes, what you describe can, on occasion, be applied to bipolar 1 disorder.

According to the DSM V, in order to meet the criteria for a diagnosis of bipolar 1, a person must have had at least one manic episode lasting a week, or necessitating a hospital admission in their life-time. The manic episode may have been preceded by and may be followed by hypo-manic or major depressive episodes. It is not necessary to have had any depressive episodes to diagnose bipolar 1 disorder.

There is a lot of publicity (usually bad) around bipolar these days. Many people assume they have the illness. The online website *Quora*, for example, has a topic on bipolar disorder and many people who are interested in this topic begin to think the symptoms apply to them.

It is not possible to diagnose yourself with bipolar disorder no matter how convinced you are you have all the symptoms. Completing one of the multitudes of bipolar quizzes online may not be accurate. The only way to be certain is to get a proper diagnosis from a qualified health professional.

First, they will rule out any physical illnesses that might be causing similar symptoms. Then they will talk with you about your history and assess your situation according to their knowledge and expertise.

If you are concerned that you might have bipolar, or any other mental illness, it would wise to make an appointment with your doctor and get a proper diagnosis.

Can bipolar affect your judgement?

I have bipolar disorder and would have said there is nothing wrong with my judgement, but the last time this question came up on Quora I had to reconsider. I have always thought of myself as a logical person who thought things through before doing them.

Unfortunately, I have to admit bipolar can affect my judgement during the manic and the depressive phases of my illness. The only time my judgement isn't impaired is in the normal (euthymic) phases in between.

When depressed I think I am not fit to live and judge myself mercilessly about all the mistakes I have made in my lifetime. I look back and think my life has been a total failure. I constantly ruminate over things that might have happened, but did not actually take place. I also cannot stop thinking about why I made certain choices in my past even if they turned out well.

Now that is not logical, is it? Yet, that is what I think about and nobody can dissuade me otherwise when I am in a depressed mood.

My judgement was really impaired when I married, but I don't know for sure if I can blame that on bipolar. I certainly made some poor decisions when deciding to marry my three husbands and have nobody else to blame but myself. My bipolar was under control with my first two marriages, but ruined my third.

On the other hand, when I am manic, I not only think I have never been happier, but that the world is a better place with me in it. I think I am Ms. Wonderful. I do not see things clearly at all, and often get annoyed with people because they seem to speak and move so slowly. I also make a lot of rash decisions and take terrible risks that I wouldn't normally take. And I say things to people I later regret.

So, sadly, I have to admit that I am illogical and my judgements are skewed when trapped in my bipolar mood swings. If this is like you, don't blame yourself, blame bipolar!

Should bipolar disorder be called tripolar disorder since there is a stable state?

Well, that is interesting. I haven't heard it mentioned before. I thought it was totally impossible as there can only be two poles, surely? One is the North Pole and the other one the South Pole, so to speak. This makes a great deal of sense when it comes to bipolar disorder. At one end of the pole is depression and at the other end is mania.

I considered the term tripolar and realized what you are referring to was the point at which a person with bipolar is well or normal between episodes. But, of course, the reason for this is generally because the medication is actually working and a person can cope with life for a time until the next episode inevitably comes around.

However, I consulted Dr. Google and was shocked to find a few entries on tri-polar disorder! The general consensus of opinion is that it is not an official, clinical diagnosis but a pseudo-psychological term coined for a person who has symptoms of borderline personality disorder combined with symptoms of bipolar. It is a particularly vexing personality disorder that clinicians find both fascinating and frustrating.

Here are the symptoms as described:

- Fear of abandonment.
- Identity disturbance.
- Suicidality or self-harm.
- Mood instability.
- Emptiness.
- Paranoia.
- Rage.
- Blaming.
- Emotional sensitivity.
- Critical.
- Dishonest and secretive.

There is no cause or cure given, only a suggestion of psychotherapy for treatment.

What are the disadvantages of having bipolar?

The problem I have with this question is that I can't think of any advantages to having bipolar disorder. None.

If I were to talk about all the disadvantages, I could go on for pages and pages. But here is a short list:

When you are young bipolar has a way of messing up your life with drugs, alcohol and sex. People in mania often do an enormous amount of all of these things. The drinking and drugging are bad enough, especially as you can die! But the sexual element in bipolar mania or hypomania can easily cause you a lot of long-term problems with STDs, unwanted pregnancies, infertility, or broken relationships.

Young people in school have a particularly hard time with their school work, particularly if they have depression. This can mean long absences, or feeling terrible if you do indeed manage to get to school and study.

When people go to University, they have the same problems only more so as a lot is at stake when you are paying for a good education.

Then, in your work, you have a very hard time getting on with people because they cannot understand where you are coming from. Sometimes you are miserable and other times you are so excitable they can't fathom what you are so happy about.

Getting on with the boss is often more difficult. Doing the work is nigh impossible. When it becomes apparent, after about 20 jobs, that you are unable to keep a job, you need to plead with the State to give you a pittance to live on. If anybody thinks the State keeps you in luxury, I can assure you they are dead wrong.

Relationships; you may as well kiss them good-bye. Before you know it all your relatives have turned their backs on you and you no longer see your so-called friends for dust. Bipolar is a relationship killer.

That rolls over into marriage. 90% of marriages where one partner has bipolar fail! That is a terrible statistic, isn't it? When you start out with 'in sickness and in health,' all seems fine, but when the person with bipolar is on their sixth hospital admission the going gets tough.

When depressed, people with bipolar are no fun to be around. Others have no idea what to do to make them feel better. The fact that no amount of cheering them up helps begins to resonate when the person refuses to get well. This is not good for marriages at all.

Mania is even worse. Who knows when they will be out there at the casino gambling away the mortgage money, or hopping in and out of bed with strangers? Nobody can tell. And what about all the arguments and screaming matches? All that is part and parcel of mania. Many people alienate their partners and the marriage fails. Trying to stop mania is like trying to stop a runaway train. Even if you stand on the tracks, nothing will stop it. The person with bipolar mania just runs you down.

Oh, and I should point out that bipolar is a potentially fatal disease. Seeing as approx. 13% to 22% of people with bipolar do in fact kill themselves it is not something to ignore. Trying to live with the constant merry-go-round of mood swings will break anybody, and sometimes the only viable solution is death for some people.

What have I missed out? So many things, too many to mention.

I think that short list will give you some idea of the disadvantages of having bipolar.

PART TWO
Coping with bipolar

I've just been diagnosed with bipolar 2 and am scared. What should I do?

Congratulations on having a diagnosis. That may seem strange, but it takes at least ten years on average to get a true diagnosis for bipolar disorder. It is usually a number of years of mental illness with the wrong medications before a conclusion can be reached. At least with a diagnosis you are half way to getting better.

Also, you seem to have accepted your diagnosis which is great. It takes most people months, even years, to accept a diagnosis of bipolar as it is not something anybody would wish on themselves. As you probably know, there is still considerable stigma surrounding this illness.

The first thing I would advise you to do is study this illness so you know what to expect. Bipolar is a very complex disorder, but you can search the Internet or buy books on the subject. You might like to get a subscription to a magazine called BP which has many interesting articles and letters from people who are living with the illness.

When you are armed with information, you will find that things begin to make sense to you. Remember to take your medications regularly. Use an alarm, or put them in a medication organizer, anything to make sure you take them correctly and at the same time each day. Without medication you are almost certain to make this illness worse.

Then you need to seek therapy of some description. Therapy is always advised along with medication for bipolar as there are so many challenges to be faced every day. There are a number of therapies to choose from, but many people swear by Cognitive Behavioral Therapy (CBT) for bipolar disorder. If this does not suit you, you might try talk therapy as you need a lot of support with this illness.

If I were you, I would do mood charts every day so that you can identify your mood swings before they arise. You can find many different mood charts online. Being prepared is always better than getting sick. Bipolar is a sneaky illness, though, and even with the best will in the world you will find you are sometimes surprised when your mood changes.

Pay great attention to your lifestyle. It is not enough to just pop a pill and talk to a therapist. You are responsible for your illness. It is your illness and nobody else's. It is up to you to play your part in staying well. Pay particular attention to sleep, diet, exercise and sunshine.

Late night parties are no longer possible without risking mood swings. Also, irregular bed times for any reason will not work. You need to get a sleep schedule going. Go to bed and wake up at the same time each day. Try not to take naps in the day time because they could interfere with your sleep.

Be sure to pay attention to diet. You will need a well-balanced diet to stay well. Also be sure to keep moving. Exercise is great for the endorphins when you are depressed, and if you can do it outside you will get the benefit of the sun's rays. I know exercise is the last thing you want to do when you are depressed, but even a ten-minute walk around the block will benefit you no end.

Over all, you need to make taking care of yourself your full-time job. Study all you can and try to build up a good support system for when times get tough. We all need someone to share our burdens, and more so with bipolar. If your family and friends seem as though they may be of help, arm them with literature that you have printed out on line. Then give them time to ask questions.

If you make a big effort, you will overcome this illness and lead a happy life. There is no cure for Bipolar, but it can be managed.

Do you sometimes feel as if you are faking bipolar?

When you have bipolar disorder, it is very common to think you are faking the illness. Many people will tell you that they feel this way, and it is a very uncomfortable feeling.

I understand this all too well because I have been through it myself. I could even say that it applies to me much of the time, even to this day. Admitting that you have bipolar disorder at all is difficult for many people, then when they get the right treatment, they begin to wonder if the diagnosis was correct.

The reason for this is your medications are working correctly, as they are designed to do. If you stopped taking the medications you would likely be very ill, then you would know for sure that you definitely do have bipolar disorder.

Don't do this to find out because it can be very dangerous. Many people start to feel so well on their medication routine they begin to think that they would be better off trying to cope with bipolar on their own. That's when things begin to go wrong, and you have to go back on them at a higher dose or go to the hospital.

As an experiment, I was taken off my medication in a hospital in England shortly after being diagnosed to see if I really had the illness, I presume. That was a horror story of immense proportions. They realized right away that I had bipolar when I went into mania. They put me straight back on the meds again.

I never question taking medication these days, I am just glad that there is something out there that can help me with this capricious illness.

What happens to people with bipolar when medication and therapy don't work?

It is a shame you have not got the help you need. You are one of the unlucky ones who doesn't respond well to treatment. I think there are more people in that category than we think. But don't give up, try WRAP (Wellness Recovery Action Plan.)

WRAP has been around for many years and is being taught internationally because it works. It takes a bit of effort on your part to understand the theory and follow it to the letter, but it can certainly improve your life if you stick to its teachings.

If you can prevent your symptoms of depression and mania you will be far better off than just trying to treat them. WRAP is all about prevention. Knowing the things that cause your mood swings is invaluable. You can learn to identify your triggers and avoid them, or at least handle them to your advantage.

WRAP also shows you how you can recognize a mood swing before it gets worse. You can work on noticing when things are worsening and take action. Then, if things get really bad, you will have a personal crisis plan which you will have worked on when you were well.

Also, I am not convinced therapy doesn't work. Something tells me you have not found the right therapist, even if you have tried many different ones. You need someone you can trust and open up to. There are thousands of therapists out there and not all therapists are suitable for everyone. You sometimes you need to kiss a lot of frogs before you find the prince. Don't give up on therapy. Find somebody who can help you.

How can I tell people i'm bipolar without them stigmatizing me?

First of all, stop telling yourself that you are bipolar. You are not bipolar; you are uniquely you who has a diagnosis of bipolar. It doesn't change who you are when you are well. You are a good person, like you always were, but life is tough because you have a serious illness.

Next, stop telling other people that you are bipolar. If you don't stop telling people you are bipolar, don't be surprised when they stop seeing the real you and just see this person who is bipolar.

Thirdly, always remember you are not a label. Who wants to go around carrying a label to describe themselves? Not me, not you, not anybody else. You are you, and that is enough. Throw your label in the ocean. If you don't live near the ocean, take it out with the trash. Anything you can do to get rid of that label is good. Stomp on it, if you must. Labels are very tough. It takes a lot of bad treatment to get rid of them.

Next, realize you are just a person who is trying to live in this mixed-up world. You are no better or worse than anybody else. We all have to suffer every day, if we have bipolar, that is surely enough?

Lastly, other people like nothing better than to gossip. They don't care who they gossip about, or whether it is true or not. You can be sure after they have told a few people about you it will not be true at all. As long as they have somebody to tell your story to, they are happy.

If you want stigma, it is out there just waiting for someone to throw it at. Stop creating problems for yourself.

How can I battle bipolar and become successful?

That is a very tall order indeed. I have bipolar 1 and never did all the things that I wanted to do. The very worst part of this illness, I think, is something that nobody mentions. When you reach a certain age, you look back and say, "What a mess this illness has made of my life."

Bipolar has a way of messing with just about everything - family, friends, job, career, marriage, kids, and everything else in between.

When you are depressed, you can't work or have a normal relationship with anybody. You feel terrible all the time and lose all incentive to do anything. And, worse, other people get frustrated with you. They just want you to snap out of it and be well again. They don't realize if you could snap out of it, you would have done so already. You didn't ask for this illness.

Many people say horrible things to you when you are depressed which make you even more miserable. Others just leave.

Then there are all the risks you take in mania. Will you ever recover from the embarrassment of shouting at your mother, or your best friend? What will you do now that your business has gone belly up? What should you do about all those sexual partners you had? You know what I mean?

I think it all depends on how old you are now, what you want to be successful at, and how motivated you are to overcome your difficulties. If you are on the winning side of all those things, you won't have too much trouble. But if you are like many people with bipolar, you will not be able to work full-time, if at all. Part-time work may be more realistic, but even then, it may be too taxing.

Assess your life - how old are you? What are your hopes and dreams? How can you go about achieving them? Make a big chart to hang on the wall. Plan your one month, one year, even five-year goals and strive to make them work for you. Anything that will spur you on is good.

Take baby steps, think before you rush in and make big decisions. Talk it over with somebody first. Think realistically, ask yourself if this is something you really want and are able to cope with when you are depressed, manic, or anxious?

On the other hand, you could be the latest entrepreneur to hit the streets. Hundreds of people in history, and today, have bipolar and have risen to the top of their fields - check it out online.

However, if all this is just too much for you, do not berate yourself, do not put yourself down. The best thing to do is to change your goals and make them more accessible to you. Then they will be much more attainable. Even if they are not quite the thing you first had in mind, completing a small goal is better than none at all.

For example, say you want to be an R.N. (like me) but the hours and the studying are just too much for you - bipolar saps your energy and concentration, as you know. Then maybe don't aim as high as doing your four-year degree course, stay in the nursing field but work in a doctor's office, nursing home, or maybe even work for an agency and nurse people who are unable to leave their home. That can be very satisfying.

It is sad, but sometimes we have to accept that certain things are too taxing for our bipolar brain and will more than likely make us ill. It is better to take smaller steps than to be ill in the hospital with your next manic or depressive episode.

How do you deal with years lost to bad mental health?

This is the very thing that most people know nothing about. In fact, I think it is the worst thing of all. My life has been a bipolar nightmare, one way and another, and lost time is the hardest thing to bear.

You get to a certain age and can't help looking back and wondering what on earth you have accomplished in your lifetime. The age at which you look back makes a big difference because if you are young, you have a much better chance of making up for lost time. When you are old, like me, it is depressing in itself, or downright infuriating.

As far as I know, we only get one chance at life and it is your fault if you waste it. Yet with an illness like bipolar what chance do you get? I have to admit bipolar was in control for years and it nearly ruined my life.

I was lucky to have a good therapist who encouraged me to make up for lost time. I returned to university, wrote a book of poems, wrote a novel, learned to draw, went on Quora and am now writing another book. All thanks to him and his faith in me.

But when I look back to the beginning of my adult life, I can see that I could have made it in several different fields if I had been well. I had to leave many good jobs due to depression, mania, anxiety or panic attacks. Those things have plagued me all my life. It is not enough to try to explain yourself when things go wrong. When people are paying for your services, their sympathy only goes so far.

I never had a problem with interviews; I could get any job I chose. When it came to the work, though, my illness would rear its ugly head and I would have to leave. My best job was as a marketing manager in a large hospital group. I was thrilled when I got that job. I managed four months then became very ill with depression and my dream came crashing down around me.

If you are looking back on your life and want to know how to deal with the lost years, I would highly recommend grieving your loss. And it is a loss. A huge loss. Losing your life's dreams and aspirations is one of the biggest losses known to mankind.

If you can go to therapy all the better, but doing it on your own may be enough. It will more than likely involve a lot of crying. That is okay. We all need to cry when we have lost something precious, like our life! It is natural and will heal in the end.

How much has bipolar ruined your relationships?

If I look back over my bipolar life, all 57 years of it, I can see that it has wrecked most of my relationships be they with family, friends, colleagues, or marital partners. If you don't control this illness the best way you can, it will wreck all your dreams and make your life miserable. Bipolar is an amazing relationship wrecker.

Unfortunately, even with the best medication routine, the symptoms can sometimes squeak through and cause you problems. That's why you need to constantly monitor your progress in order to stay on top of it. Keep a mood chart and share it with your psychiatrist on your next visit.

I can see now that my negative thoughts led to my emotions which in turn led to my faulty behavior in my relationships. I am shocked and humbled to think of all the crazy things I have said and done in the past and realize now that this has ruined so many things for me.

This was not apparent at the time, and I always blamed my behavior. Now I realize that I should have been working harder on my thought processes which in turn would have corrected my behavior. This is where Cognitive Behavioral Therapy (CBT) is very useful as it teaches you how to change your negative thought patterns. People don't often recognize negativity in themselves, or they have no idea how to change it.

Unfortunately, when you have this illness, you are often unable to put yourself in another person's shoes. You cannot fully understand why people react to you the way they do. Even if you think you are being the ideal partner or friend, people sometimes have difficulty relating to you in a normal way.

It would be nice to be able to go back and do it all again with some people, but that is not an option. However, now I am on the right medication, I can think clearly, so am in charge of my behavior to a large extent. Even so, there are still some people who seem to have a hard time being with me and I have no idea why. Perhaps they would have a hard time being with me even if I didn't have this illness.

What problems have you faced with a history of bipolar?

My bipolar disorder began when I was fifteen in the 1960s, although at the time neither I, nor anybody else, knew that I had this illness. I was with my dying mother in the hospital when it suddenly occurred to me that I should not be sitting there doing nothing, I should be entertaining all the other patients in their beds. I chatted away to this one and that one, doing silly impressions, laughing uproariously, getting so excited in my new found mania that I could easily have done a few one-handed cartwheels around the long, open-plan ward in London.

From then on, my life has been one-long merry-go-round from hell.

My constant mood swings:

For years my anti-depressants did not respond to treatment because, in those days, doctors did not realize that these medications can cause a manic reaction in people with bipolar. It was one week of sobbing under the covers totally unable to look after a cat, let alone myself, followed by another few days of ranting and raving and shouting and screaming at anybody who dared to come near me. Then another couple of weeks of misery, followed by another day or two of stripping off in public, driving at 90 mph through town, racking up debt buying duplicates, or even triplicates of anything that took my fancy. I had quite a collection of purses in those days. And my book collection would have impressed the local library.

Jobs:

Who can work and try to cope with the vagaries of bipolar disorder? Only a robot. I counted back the other day and discovered I have had 22 jobs in my lifetime, many of them really desirable, lucrative jobs. However, anybody with this illness will gladly tell you that it is nigh impossible to try to work while you are shaking from head to toe with anxiety, running in the restroom five times a day with panic attacks, sitting almost comatose at your desk because your head is full of cotton wool when you're depressed, skipping around the office singing stupid songs, or thumping your fist on your boss's desk, screaming bloody murder in his startled face when you are manic.

It is out the door with you, Sally Alter. Bring the company car back tomorrow.

Diagnosis:

After ten years of this crazy life style, I read a book called *Mood Swings* and raced to my doctor to tell him I had bipolar disorder (or manic depression as it was called at the time.) He put me on Lithium, then three weeks later I was in the hospital. Apparently, Lithium had caused hypothyroidism so I would now have to take Synthroid for the rest of my life. Whilst in hospital, I was taken off Lithium and I literally went crazy.

I was totally barred from group therapy because I got up and almost attacked somebody, screaming and shouting at them because they had said something that upset me. And when my brother and his wife came to visit me, I threw the box of chocolates they brought for me on the floor. I was quickly put back on Lithium to quell the mania. As is considered 'normal' with this cursed illness, the moment your secret is out, all your friends, relatives, colleagues and neighbors vanish into thin air, never to be seen again.

Marriages:

Who wants to be married to a wild beast that throws things around the room, pulls the chandelier down from the ceiling, paces up and down for hours, cries for weeks, and hasn't got the energy to cook a meal? I don't think so.

I managed to get through three husbands with no problem at all. Although, I would have to say that I have a distinct knack of attracting men that somehow realize you are a total wreck, even when you manage to get it together in front of their mother. The whole marriage barely gets off the ground. I have come to the conclusion that marriage is definitely a two-way street. Putting up with all the smoking, drinking, drugging, gambling, womanizing, stealing, lying, manipulating etc. (the combination of three errant men) would be enough to blow the halo off a saint. And I was no saint.

Mental hospitals:

Not only do I know most of the hospitals in London, since moving to Texas I know most of the hospitals here, as well. In fact, I have spent fourteen months of my life locked up in these hospitals as if I was a criminal. I have even been driven there in handcuffs in various police cars. Everybody knows me in these hospitals, and they usually duck when I come in bristling with mania, or simply ignore me when I am depressed. Being escorted to the ER covered in blood from a suicide attempt is another story that people in my position will understand all too well. Bipolar is great for taking you out of your misery on a permanent basis if that is what you want.

However, now that I have found the right combination of medications, I am here to tell you that I am enjoying life more than I ever thought possible. When times get tough, and they will, always realize that there is hope out there when it comes to bipolar disorder.

What do people with bipolar wish others understood about it?

Well, I have always been told I should write a book about bipolar disorder because it has been the story of my life and responsible for most of my failings. And now I can see that even that question required a book length response.

I will summarize a few points:

- Bipolar disorder is not fun.

- It is not something one wishes upon oneself.

- It has nothing to do with personality or character.

- It is a physical illness likely caused by an imbalance in brain chemistry.

- Bipolar disorder is classified as a severe mood disorder.

- It is an illness with a strong genetic link.

- It may also be brought about by trauma, especially in childhood.

- It is often worsened by stress.

- Bipolar disorder usually starts in late teens, early twenties, but is becoming more common in children and people in late adulthood.

- There are two common types of the illness, bipolar 1 and bipolar 2.

- Neither 1 or 2 is fun.

- Bipolar 1 is diagnosed when a person has experienced at least one manic episode in their life time. They may or may not have had depressive episodes.

- Bipolar 2 is diagnosed when a person has experienced at least one episode of hypomania as well as depressive episodes.

- People with major depressive disorder (MDD) do not experience hypomania or mania because they have a unipolar mood disorder.

- Bipolar 1 and 2 have similar symptoms, but bipolar 2 does not rise to the point of mania.

- Each illness is awful.

- People with bipolar 2 are more likely to be productive during hypomanic episodes. They are more likely to be able to lead normal lives than those with bipolar 1.

- People with bipolar 1 can become so ill that they are unable to function at all.

- People with bipolar 1 are often admitted to the hospital. Rarely in bipolar 2.

- Bipolar 1 mania and depression can lead to psychosis. In fact, around 60% of all people with bipolar will experience at least one episode of psychosis in their life time.

- There is no cure for bipolar disorder, but it is treatable.

- The main treatment is medication - mood-stabilizers and often anti-depressants and anti-psychotics.

- Medications often need to be changed, and some people are medicine resistant.

- People get into trouble when they try to stop taking medication because they think they are well. Then they realize the reason they were well was because they were taking the medication.

- The other treatment recommended is ongoing therapy.

- Peer groups are also highly recommended.

- Anxiety, panic attacks, and many other similar illnesses are common in people with bipolar disorder.

- There is still a lot of stigma surrounding this illness which makes it doubly hard for people trying to cope with its symptoms.

- The reason for stigma is fear. And the reason for fear is ignorance. The answer to both is education.

There, that's a short list of general information about bipolar disorder.

Now I shall summarize what life is like for somebody trying to cope with bipolar disorder:

- You can be pretty certain that nobody will understand what is happening to you as you don't even understand it yourself.

- Living life on a roller-coaster never gets easier, and often gets worse with age.

- The uncertainty of when or if an episode will strike is horrible.

- Bipolar disorder will definitely mess with all areas of your life so you had better be prepared for it.

- It will try to mess with your education making it very difficult to concentrate at college. People often drop out of college due to bipolar disorder.

- It will do a number on your friends and relatives, and you can be sure you will lose many or all of your friends and relatives due to this illness.

- Marriage is really touch and go. Making a success of a marriage requires an understanding partner. But even with the best will in the world, not all partners will be able to tolerate how their partner behaves.

- It is very difficult to live with a person with bipolar disorder.

- There is a strong possibility that children of that marriage will have bipolar disorder in the future which makes having children a very uncertain decision.

- Work will be a very big challenge, especially getting there on time when depressed, and being able to make sense of the job when you get there because you cannot think clearly no matter how hard you try.

- Getting on with colleagues will more than likely be an enormous challenge as people have little to no understanding of this illness.

- The decision whether to tell is yours, but you can guarantee that if you tell people you have this illness, they will look down on you or treat you like an imbecile.

- When you have bipolar, it will be very difficult, if not impossible, to remain in a job. In fact, many people are unable to work at all.

- That is why it is rare to see a rich person with this illness unless they have a lot of help from others.

- When you are in a severe depressive episode you can expect to be exhausted all the time with no energy to even brush your teeth, and sometimes your energy gets so low that you are unable to get out of bed.

- You can expect to either sleep for about 16–18 hours a day, or be unable to sleep at all. And your appetite and your weight will suffer, too.

- The worst part of depression is the feelings of guilt, sadness, hopelessness, helplessness and a general lack of motivation to do the things you once enjoyed. And there will be tears of frustration when trying to do things that others find easy.

- Then there is the loneliness, the anger, and even the rage, and the constant thoughts of death and suicide? Spending all day lost in thoughts of how you should kill yourself is just not fun at all. And this goes on and on for the duration of your depression.

- The suicide rate in people with this illness is much higher than the normal population. 13% to 22% of people actually do commit suicide and another almost 50% make at least one attempt.

- Moving from chair to bed, then bed to chair all day is something you come to think of as your normal way of life because when you are depressed you can see no end in sight.

- When you are depressed, you can almost certainly expect somebody to say inappropriate things to you, like, "Cheer up" or "Pull yourself together" or "You should get out and meet people" or "You're only making yourself feel worse sitting indoors all day."

- These things are all very well, but if you could do even one of them you would have already done it. And people telling you to "snap out of it" just intensifies the guilt.

- Hypo-mania is quite a relief after a long depression because you suddenly have all the energy in the world. You are productive, creative and can tackle many projects at once.

- But then there is always the possibility that this wonderful euphoria can quickly get out of hand and you will embarrass yourself and everybody else around you.

- You will not be aware that you are manic when in mania and will not listen to people who try to tell you that you are ill. How can you be ill when you feel so well - stupid?

- In mania you are very likely to say and do things you will bitterly regret later. You will have to keep apologizing to everybody, and many people will not want to be near you ever again.

- Mania can lead to huge shopping sprees, road rage, gambling, impulsive sexual encounters and all manner of risk-taking endeavors which will be bitterly regretted later.

- Psychosis is not perceptible to you either because you can no longer tell reality from fiction. It is frankly terrifying. A life filled with hallucinations and delusions is terrible.

- And being in a mental hospital means losing your freedom and all sense of who you are and how you manage your life.

- Some people do well from a hospital stay, but others do not.

- Then there's the bill! There's always the bill even though people know you have no means of paying it because you cannot work.

- God help you if you can manage a life on the line.

- The very worst thing about bipolar disorder is that when you reach a certain age, you will undoubtedly look back on your life and feel that you have been a complete failure. All the hopes and dreams you had for your life when you were young have simply evaporated into thin air.

I don't know how much more you want to know because I am already deep into chapter two of my book of bipolar.

What is high functioning bipolar disorder?

High functioning bipolar disorder describes someone who is autonomous. This means that they are capable of living their own life without practical help from others. If you can take care of your bills, grocery shopping, cooking, cleaning, and everyday affairs then you are high functioning according to this definition.

A person who needs somebody else to advocate for them, and show them how to do the basic things in life, is not high functioning. They really need to be watched closely and assisted with practically everything. Many people with bipolar who are not high functioning live in group homes and rely on others for everything even to the point of dispensing their medications so that there is no confusion.

Others, who are able to live alone in the community, need some help if it's only to take the dog to the vet as many people with bipolar are unable to drive. Medications have side effects, especially anti-psychotics, and these can be very debilitating.

The problem that high functioning people sometimes run into is when things go wrong and they are in the throes of a bad episode, they do not always receive the help they need because more is expected of them.

I have been in this situation a number of times myself, particularly when experiencing psychosis. I can no longer think clearly and need a lot of assistance. I have ended up in hospital on many occasions and it has created untold problems for me because nobody is at home to feed my cats, pay my rent, or start up my car in the driveway so that I don't get a flat battery. Not to mention all the perishables going bad in the fridge.

The way I cope with this is to recruit people who will be able to step in if I am taken to the hospital, but it is amazing how difficult it is to be able to rely on anybody. The person who happily took care of my cats for years, moved away last year and it has been difficult finding someone reliable to replace her. All I can hope for is the person who says they will come to feed my cats will do so, or I stay well enough to avoid going to the hospital.

So being high functioning has its good and bad points, but on the whole I would much rather be autonomous.

Is it better to mix with the mentally ill or the mentally well?

I attended a clinic for the mentally ill and mentally retarded for years. This clinic has many activities like peer groups every day, various workshops, dances and dinners on holidays, and a meeting place where people with mental illness can socialize. There are social workers who help the best they can.

In the past I attended all these things, then began to develop an aversion to these groups. I realized that I did not want to identify with people with mental illness any longer because it was preventing me from getting well.

To simplify, let us look at this situation as archetypes:

Wounded child – The person who is mentally ill.

Rescuer – Social Workers and people who want to help.

The Wounded Child is one who cannot seem to let go of the past and all the terrible things that have happened in their lives. They talk about their traumas, often physically and sexually, and how they have had to suffer at the hands of others for years. They can see no hope for a brighter future, but make little to no effort to help themselves.

This sets the stage for the Rescuer. "Ah, here is a Wounded Child that needs my help." The Rescuer rushes in and advocates for the Wounded Child. He takes them by the hand, makes phone calls for them, takes them to appointments, fills in forms, pays their bills, and generally enables them.

There are those that want to remain Wounded Children. And there are the Rescuers who get paid in most cases to help when things go wrong - which they inevitably do.

Having given up the role of the Wounded Child and the Rescuer altogether, I now mix with people who are mentally well. I never tell them I have an illness at all. In other words, I never show them my Wounded Child, so they never have to take on the burden of Rescuing me.

I hear of people who have told their families and friends about their illnesses and are surprised to learn that they are either ostracized altogether or treated like a moron who needs permanent care. If you are unfortunate enough to have a mental illness, it is up to you to educate yourself and do everything within your power to cope with your illness and mix with normal society. This is a mammoth task, but who said it would be easy?

I do have to say, though, that certain peer groups are often helpful to people who need them. They are just not for me.

Can you be hospitalized many times and still work and be successful?

I have bipolar 1 and have been repeatedly hospitalized over the years. Fourteen months of my life have been wasted behind bars in mental hospitals, but I can honestly say that I now have a happy life and am successful by my estimation.

I no longer have to work because I am retired. but I did spend most of my life successfully furthering my nursing career. It was not without difficulties, but I managed to keep my moods under control by leading a healthy lifestyle.

I found it very helpful to work the night shift because there wasn't so much going on. There were no doctors or therapists entering the unit because patients were asleep. However, not everybody is suited to night work as it does alter your biological clock.

I understand your frustration as bipolar is hell to live with, but you can live a good life and be successful in your career. Most people with bipolar have to work, but some have a very hard time with keeping a job for any length of time.

One thing to bear in mind is to work at a career than doesn't involve much stress. If you were in sales, for example, you would find it very difficult to be able to do your job when feeling depressed.

If it becomes too difficult for you, you might try reducing your hours or changing careers. Anything to make it easier. Just don't fall off the horse as it is difficult to climb back up again.

The key is to get the right psychiatrist who will prescribe a cocktail of meds that will work for you. Sometimes, we have to try many meds and side effects can be a nuisance, but finding the right combination is essential if you have bipolar.

Be sure to check out any new medication before taking it. Be selective as to what you put in your body. Always be one step ahead of the curve. It is your life you are dealing with. Being well is paramount. Don't settle for second best.

Also, bear in mind that taking meds is only part of staying well with bipolar. You really need to put in the work yourself which means keeping a regular bedtime and waking up time, eating a proper diet, exercising and getting out in the sunshine. If you work at a challenging job, you might like to learn to do some relaxation exercises which will help to keep you calm when problems arise.

I have also found psychotherapy invaluable, and attribute a lot of my success to my psychotherapist. I have been seeing him for many years now as I believe therapy should be ongoing with bipolar. The day-to-day problems are endless.

Life goes on and we have to cope the best way we can.

My friend says I am toxic because I have bipolar. What should I do?

Whenever I hear the word toxic, I think of someone with toxic fumes coming out of their head. They could be a monster or an ogre. It seems quite ridiculous to me. The word toxic, as pertaining to others, is a fairly new word and is not a label that people wear around their necks. To say somebody is toxic is an insult, not a fact.

A person who is termed toxic has some of the following traits:

- They exhaust a person emotionally.

- They intimidate them.

- They try to control them.

- They are jealous and play the victim.

- They give backhanded compliments.

- They are over defensive.

People talk about their toxic mother, or their toxic spouse, but that doesn't mean it is a diagnosis. It is just a word, an ugly word. Of course, it is true there are people who are abusive and have always been abusive. You could label them toxic if you wanted to.

To apply that word to a person who has bipolar is just plain wrong. As I said it is an insult, and the person saying that to you is no friend of yours. They only want to upset you and they have obviously achieved that.

Bipolar is an illness. It is not something you can help. Nobody wishes an illness on themselves, especially one like bipolar that can cause you a lifetime of suffering. I can imagine how hurt you must be because of this.

If I was you, I would quickly cut all ties with that person and have nothing more to do with them. You don't need to explain yourself or your illness to them. It is none of their business. But you do need to get away from them because, if you want to use their terminology, you could call them the toxic person out of the pair of you.

I have bipolar which makes me seem rude at times. Should I tell my co-workers about my mental illness?

This has been a problem for me many times in the past. To tell or not to tell?

It seems simple - if you tell people, they will understand and make allowances for you, but I have found nothing could be further from the truth. People do not understand, and they do not want to make allowances for you either.

The average person in the street has no idea about mental illness unless it affects them or somebody close to them. People have no problem with accepting physical illnesses because they can see what is wrong with the person, or at least know of someone with the particular disease in question.

Mental illnesses are just not like that. You can't see what is wrong, and they come with a great deal of stigma attached to them.

People generally do not understand the workings of the brain, and more so the mind. In fact, the majority of people do not want to know about these things. There is a tremendous fear in some that if you are sick with a mental illness, they might catch it, as if mental illnesses are contagious. Someone once asked me if bipolar was a pandemic!

As for making allowances for you, I have found that will not happen. Instead, the average person, especially if they are afraid of catching your particular illness, will give you a very wide berth. They will look down on you or make your life even more difficult than it already is.

Sometimes people, despite their best intentions, seem to want to punish people with mental illnesses as if it was their fault. Mental illness is not something you wish upon yourself, as you very well know.

All told, I have found that when I have shared this knowledge with people, they gossip about me, look down on me, think they are better than me, or worse, treat me with kid gloves and make me feel as if I am about to break down any minute.

Either way it is embarrassing and soul-destroying. I made up my mind a long time ago not to share this knowledge with anyone unless I had to.

I would say in most cases you have no need to tell co-workers. They do not need to know such personal details about you. I am sure if you had cancer you wouldn't want to talk about it at work.

You could well be wrong about how you appear to others. You may think you are rude, but maybe other people don't see it that way. Otherwise, you will need to do your best to eliminate that behavior altogether.

How does someone cope with bipolar if they live alone?

I have bipolar 1 with psychotic features and have lived on my own for the past twenty years. People say it is essential to have some support when you have a serious illness like bipolar, and having an understanding family and friends is definitely a great help if you need someone to talk to. Also, if you have a crisis and need to go to the hospital, it is good to know you have people to stay with you and visit during your stay. But getting that kind of support is not always easy.

If you live alone and have no family or friends to speak of, it can be difficult to manage the symptoms of bipolar on your own. Most of my family are gone, and those that have accepted my illness have little interest in understanding bipolar.

I have found that friends have not been interested in my illness, either. I have given them books to read and tried talking to them about it, but if people do not want to be supportive nothing can make them.

I do have a case worker at a local clinic who is there at the end of the telephone line should I need her. The problem with that is you have to be sick during the week because clinic staff do not work at the weekends.

Of course, like any employee, case workers change jobs all the time. I have had at least fifteen case workers over the years, and they have become interchangeable. Also, they are only there to give practical advice, most of which I know already because I have had bipolar all my life.

I do have a wonderful therapist, but he is not available outside of office hours either. I have called him at odd times when I have had a crisis, but I do not make a habit of it.

Getting help from strangers is better than no help at all, and I do call a crisis line for somebody to talk to sometimes, but that is far less satisfying as they do not know my circumstances. Hoping to get some support from others is unreliable at best.

Living alone with bipolar is very difficult. You need to be able to advocate for yourself, live a healthy lifestyle, and plan ahead for every eventuality.

If you can make a Crisis Plan when you are well, that will be helpful. Then, when you are in a crisis situation, you won't need to make hasty decisions about what to do and where to go.

How important is managing stress in bipolar disorder?

Managing stress in bipolar disorder is paramount to staying well. It is a fact that stress of any kind makes bipolar worse, and sometimes it can cause the illness to spiral out of control altogether. The person sinks into an intractable depression and may become so ill they end up in the hospital.

I have bipolar and avoid stress like the plague. The way I do this is to concentrate on my triggers and either avoid them altogether, or accept that some things are out of my control.

One summer we had a hail storm in my town. The roof and the side of my house were severely damaged. I did all I could to remedy the situation, but only received three quotes from local contractors. None of them compared with the amount of money the insurance company had given me. I then got in touch with another four contractors and had to wait for their quotes to come in. Two weeks later I had not heard a word. This was a very stressful situation indeed, made worse because I live alone.

I knew I had to do something about the roof and the house, but I was getting nowhere. What could I do? Well, I could have sat down and cried. I could even have ended up in the hospital if I let the stress overwhelm me. Instead, I decided to accept that this was the situation and I was at the mercy of other people.

A few days later, I called all the people again to see what had happened to their quotes. I was aware that this was a big problem as there are few roofers in my town, and even fewer who want to repair the house at the same time as the roof.

Acceptance is key. I accepted that the wheels turned very slowly indeed. I had done all I could and my frustration wasn't going to change the matter. It took another month before I managed to get someone to replace my roof. Someone else had to repair the damage to the outside of the house.

This could have played havoc with my bipolar, but I took care of myself during that time. I made sure I slept and ate well, and I did relaxation and creative visualization exercises. I also took time out to breathe.

How can flying be beneficial to someone with Bipolar disorder?

I am not sure where you heard that, but it is a known fact that travel plays havoc with a person's biological clock if you have bipolar. If you are well, you can adjust accordingly, but if you have bipolar it will often throw you off completely, especially when traveling across different time zones.

I have bipolar and have traveled to many places in the world. The main problem I had was with my medication. If you are traveling a long way and have to take medication on the plane, it is easy to get confused. Day can seem like night when you are in flight. It can be very unsettling.

Traveling to Australia three times was terrible. It never got any better. I found it impossible to get my medication regime right during the nineteen-hour flight, and could barely get out of bed when I got there because I was so depressed. Flying to Malta was really bad as my anxiety got the better of me and I could barely leave the hotel room.

But the worst holiday of all was in Costa Rica. I found the coach trip I went on was full of couples and friends and I was very lonely. The moment I arrived at the first hotel, I went into a sudden hypo-manic episode that had me laughing and dancing all around the room. I wrote copious notes in my journal about the wonderful ambience of the hotel.

Then just as suddenly, I had a panic attack and was sweating and shaking from head to foot. I wanted to leave immediately, but my mind was so muddled I couldn't decide what to do. It was an impossible situation. I had no idea how to get back to the airport or how to change my flight, and the prospect of joining the coach party the next morning filled me with dread.

I had many panic attacks on that holiday and made a complete fool of myself more than once. I noticed that people avoided me and barely said, "Hello." I was so distraught I cried in my room for ages.

I completely lost it one night when all the couples went to see an active volcano erupt. It was pitch black at the top of the mountain and we had to cross a rope bridge over a gorge in the pouring rain. I could hear the river crashing over the rocks below. To say I was terrified would be an understatement. I just wanted a hand to hold so that I could get safely across the bridge without falling into a pothole. After waiting for twenty minutes in the darkness, I stupidly shouted out that I wanted to go back to the hotel. Nobody answered. The volcano erupted red flames in the distance, and I never lived down that experience.

I could go on about my various mishaps all over the world, but will leave you to imagine how ill a person can get when they have bipolar disorder, anxiety and panic. I would advise anybody with these illnesses not to go anywhere on their own. Stay with people you know who can help you when things go wrong as they will inevitably will.

Why do I switch from goal to goal? One day I want to write a book, then I get bored and switch to another goal. What is wrong with me?

In this life we are always being told that we must have a goal. It seems indecent, almost, to go through life without knowing where you are headed. People, for one reason or another, look down on others if they appear to have nothing to strive for.

We are told we should take courses on goal-directed activities; we learn to break up our goals into sizable chunks so that we can attain them. We use planners and have vision boards on our walls. We buy books and read articles on goal attainment. This is a goal-driven society, but it doesn't make it right.

If you look back in time, you will find that people just went about their lives without giving a single thought to spending all their time on trying to achieve a particular goal. Ladies in the Victorian era had their needlework, pioneers had their families and their cattle to feed and take care of. They just did what they had to do to earn a living to keep afloat. And the gentry never considered working for a living at all.

Even at the beginning of the 20th Century most people just went about their business, working every day to earn a living. Few people lived their lives with one particular goal in mind. Many men worked at blue collar jobs, got their pay on Fridays and went down to the bar to have a drink with their mates. They may have been envious of people who were better off than themselves, but they had no particular goals to improve their lot. And a large number of men went to war so the last thing on their mind was a goal.

Women stayed at home with the children and their only goal was to keep them fed and well-clothed. It is true some families wanted their children to have a good education, but in the first part of the 20th Century they were in the minority.

Now, in the 21st Century all that has changed. Men and women strive for well-paid careers and employ others to take care of the children and the house. People who have no definite goals are made to feel guilty and in the minority. How sad is that?

I used to want to write a novel, but I also wanted to paint at the same time. I thought I should choose just one goal and stick to it. It caused me agonies of indecision for years. Then I realized I could do both things at once, so I satisfied myself with that. While my husband and I traveled around the country in an RV, I managed to write that novel and sell many paintings as well as teach classes in both subjects in the campgrounds we stayed in.

Now, here I am, writing this book about bipolar, and I am happy. But it is not the goal that counts, it is the process. If you enjoy what you are doing then that should be enough.

Has your bipolar condition ever changed?

Yes, do let me give you some hope. I know bipolar is a nightmare - it has been my nightmare, and my daymare, for more than fifty years - but believe it or not there really is hope out there.

I have been through the mill one way and another; many, many hospital visits and endless weeks of sickness. I have lost jobs, relatives, friends and husbands to this awful disease. I can't tell you what else, but it is a whole lot of losses.

I could have a Garden of Remembrance with all the crosses of people I have lost. Or rather no longer want to know me.

Yet, finally, here I am, well and happy. And I have been well for a year and a half now. I feel I should whisper it unless my bad luck comes whooshing back to bite me.

But, no, here I am feeling better than I have ever felt in my life. No depression, mania, psychosis or anything else. Just feeling well. I haven't been near a hospital in ten years.

"How did you do it," you are asking, quite rightly. The answer is to find the right medication. I know, you have tried every cocktail known to man. Well, so have I. But finally, finally, the right medication for me came along and I am now well.

Doesn't matter what that medication is. No two people are alike anyway, so what works for me may not work for you. But I just want you to know there is hope out there.

PART THREE
Relationships

Why do I always want to explain my illness to people?

I always wanted to tell people about my illness like you. Perhaps I wanted them to understand and give me a break when things went wrong. The problem is there is still so much stigma attached to bipolar disorder, people mostly shrink and disappear when you start to tell them about it.

When I was manic (which was often when my meds weren't working properly) I used to want to share my personal story with the members of the congregation in my church. Once, I stood up and made a total fool of myself by telling the whole congregation I had bipolar disorder and apologized if I had offended anyone. The woman who was sitting next to me excused herself and made a hasty exit.

The congregation ignored me from that day forth. Every time I joined a group of people they would disperse very quickly and I would be left standing there on my own.

Another time, I asked a woman who I thought was my friend if she would help me over the next few days because I was feeling very ill with depression. I didn't see her for dust until a month later when she said, with a sideways glance, "I see you got through your depression".

I stayed with that church for five more years and endured more and more of this treatment. It was like having leprosy. Finally, I decided enough was enough when people got up and excused themselves when I sat down next to them. They would mumble something about wanting to say hello to a friend, then I never saw them again. Once a woman got up and said the pews on the other side were empty so she thought she would sit there!

Whilst at that church I decided to give a talk about bipolar disorder. The room was full to bursting and people asked the most ridiculous questions. Someone wanted to know if it was in the water, or in the air! And another man, a professor, no less, wanted to know if it had anything to do with the Democratic party!

I have been in mental hospitals many times, but was just forgotten by my church with no word from them whatsoever. Not a phone call, a card, or a visit. Bipolar is a very lonely illness.

I know of another woman who has bipolar disorder. She went to a church for seven years, then when she had a double mastectomy, she didn't see anybody from the congregation at all despite the fact that she had visited many people in hospital herself. She didn't get a card, let alone a bunch of flowers. This poor woman got MERSA from the hospital and had to stay in for weeks without a word from the church.

So, I would strongly advise you to keep your private business private. People do not want to know about your bipolar disorder, and they certainly won't understand it.

How can I tell my family I have bipolar?

First of all, carefully consider telling your family. People with bipolar will all tell you that they have lost innumerable family members and friends due to coming out. It is not always something that people can understand, or indeed what they want to hear about. The more people you tell, the more the risk of being ostracized.

There is something about bipolar disorder that people cannot accept. The stigma is still very strong. People now accept depression and some of the other mental illnesses, but bipolar often makes people very wary.

If you do decide it is worth telling some family members I would go on line and find something short that describes bipolar in a non-threatening way. Then print it out and give it to them to read. If they want to ask questions then you can give them the answers to the best of your ability.

I no longer tell anybody I have bipolar because I have lost many, many friends and relatives to this crushing disease.

Can someone with bipolar have a normal marriage?

That begs the question - What is normal? It is a fact that 50% of marriages end in divorce. And that applies to the general public, people who may not have any form of mental illness, let alone something as serious as bipolar.

There is no doubt that marriage with at least one bipolar partner is difficult. I have never heard of one that was 'normal'. It is a case of, "join me on the roller coaster or bring me down to earth".

Whatever else happens, if a partner has bipolar it will pose an enormous challenge in any marriage. Trying to live with one's own mood swings is a full-time job, let alone trying to make it work with a partner who is well.

I have found that it takes an exceptional person to ride the waves with their bipolar partner and float to shore unharmed. It is too much for many people.

Bipolar is a curse. It ruins many relationships. Therefore, having a successful marriage is doubly difficult. The partner has to be a saint. It is very hard to live with somebody who is depressed for weeks on end. It seems reasonable that the person can just snap out of it, but it doesn't work that way and many things can go wrong, including suicide.

Mania can be worse. How do you cope with somebody who is running up bills right, left and center, buying all kinds of things they don't need? They may max out the credit cards and raid the savings account as well. And then there are the affairs? What happens when the partner is out all night, hopping into bed with strangers? That can be a deal breaker.

Without a doubt, living with somebody who has bipolar is a huge challenge. The success rates in such marriages are horrendous - about 10%.

I have found that marriages go one of two ways. The unrelenting mood swings can either make or break a marriage. I think it is similar to losing a child in so much as it will either make the marriage stronger, or tear you apart. Marriage is a two-way street, it is true, but bipolar behavior will cause a lot of trouble.

The only way to deal with this situation is for the bipolar partner to take full responsibility for themselves and their actions. They would need to take medications and never miss a dose, get to sleep on time and eat a healthy diet.

The partner who is well would be wise to read up all they can on bipolar so that they can better understand the situation. They might also like to go to support groups for spouses of people with bipolar disorder.

If two people do these things, the marriage may have a chance of success.

How can I explain to my employer that absenteeism and tardiness are due to bipolar?

Think of this:

Your employer is the captain of a ship. All is well when the crew are in situ and doing their jobs. The ship will stay afloat and the captain will have more time to devote to the very important things that he needs to do.

I am not the captain of a ship, and I don't know what it takes to run one, but I do know that I would expect my crew to be there on time, backing me up and helping me do my job. If a member of my crew is constantly late, or is 'absent without leave', I would find it very difficult to guide my ship where I want it to go.

It's the same with you. You are a member of your employer's crew and you need to do whatever it takes to stay well. You need to be there to help him be a success. That is your job.

I know you are sick - I have bipolar myself and have suffered immeasurably - but it is not enough to keep letting your employer down. If you need time off then let him know the reason why. If you are afraid to disclose your illness, tell him that you have a mood disorder or bouts of depression. He may not understand, but at least he will know why you are off work.

Be sure you are taking good care of yourself and your illness. Make sure you are taking your medication regularly, sleeping well and eating a good diet. You could also get some exercise and get out in the sunshine as all these things are beneficial to bipolar.

But never be tardy. Always make sure you are there on time, if not before. Show a good face, be willing, and keep your job. As you probably know, jobs are hard to find, and even harder to keep when you have bipolar. So be grateful that you have a job and are earning a decent wage. Imagining that you can live comfortably off Social Security is a myth. Don't test that one out or you will be sorry.

How can I explain to people that bipolar depression is not like anything they have experienced?

I am sorry you feel depressed. I have bipolar and I know just what it is like. I can empathize with you because I have bipolar. However, somebody who doesn't have bipolar, or even mental health issues, can never understand how you feel no matter how hard they try.

All they know is they have bad moods sometimes, but they don't realize that the bad moods of bipolar are nothing like those of other people who are well. How could they?

If you met somebody who had an amputation of their leg, no matter how that person tried to explain how it felt to be an amputee, you would never understand that, would you?

It is simply not possible for people who have never experienced something to have any idea how it feels if they have not suffered it themselves.

Do you know how it feels to be blind, or deaf, or have cancer? No. How could you if you have never experienced it yourself? So, you have to realize that you will never be able to explain the depth of feeling you have to anyone.

All you can hope for is that somebody understands you have an illness which takes up all your energy. Bipolar depression leaves a person with no energy to do anything at all, and sitting around on the couch all day is just what happens.

How much has bipolar ruined your relationships, school, and work?

If I look back over my bipolar life, I can see a steady stream of chaos in my relationships, school and work. No matter how hard you try, bipolar can be the death of all the things above. If you take medication, which is a must, you may be disappointed to find your symptoms are squeaking through every so often. This makes living with this illness even more of a challenge.

I can see now that my thoughts lead to my emotions which lead to my faulty behavior. This was not apparent at the time, and I blamed only my behavior. Now I realize that I should have been working on my thought processes first because none of what I did made any sense.

I am shocked and humbled if I think back to all the crazy things I have said and done in my life, and can see that bipolar has ruined so many things for me.

Unfortunately, when you have this illness, you are often unable to put yourself in other people's shoes so cannot fully understand why other people react the way they do. Even if you think you are doing a great job, people cannot relate to you in a normal way. It is so disheartening.

I lost my relationships with most of my family and friends to this illness, along with problems in school and work. It is only now, looking back, that I can see why my behavior was unacceptable. It is not immediately obvious when it is occurring.

It would be nice to go back and do it all again but that is not an option. However, now that I am on the right medication, I can think clearly so am in charge of my behavior to a large extent. Even so, there are still some people who seem to have a hard time being with me, and I have no idea why.

As I say, bipolar disorder is the great destroyer. It smashes through your life and every dream you ever had like a wrecking ball.

In a fit of bipolar 1 rage, I cussed at my friend. Now I am sorry. How do I reconcile with him?

Many people have not heard of bipolar rage, and just as many don't think it exists. How could anybody keep losing their temper over nothing, and how could they lose control of their tongue? But that is what happens when you are in a rage. When they talk about blood boiling, it certainly feels like that.

It has nothing to do with irritability, or even anger, rage is beyond description and terrible for the person who has to suffer it - perhaps worse for the person on the receiving end of your rage. When you get in the rage cycle, it can go on for days, weeks or even months. It is exhausting. I know all about rage, and it is terrible.

Unfortunately, a lot can go wrong when you are in a rage episode, and you are sure to regret it later. The problem is that other people have feelings, and their feelings get hurt. They take offence, and you may never hear from them again. Although you did not intend to be mean to your friend, bipolar is an impulsive disorder and many things are said and done without thinking.

It is very tempting to ask for forgiveness, maybe you should, but the thing to realize is that people will react differently. Some may forgive, many others will not. I personally found that most people did not accept my apologies no matter what I did. You may be luckier.

So, go ahead, apologize from the heart to your friend, but do not be surprised if the results are disappointing. To say you need to keep an eye on your temper is useless when you are in the rage episode. The only way to cope is to keep your distance from others.

Also, be aware that rage can lead to violence, then you can be in all kinds of trouble with the law. Many people are in prison because they snapped. You don't want to be one of them. And if you harm someone, you may get a lot of hospital bills. Beware of road rage as this can cause you no end of problems. I have a tendency towards this myself and have had far too many near misses.

Is it difficult for people with bipolar to find a mate?

Relationships of any kind are always hanging in the balance when you have bipolar. You may find it hard to make friends, and you probably find it even harder to keep them. People seem to avoid you, and half the time you have no idea what you have done to offend them.

If it is difficult to maintain an ordinary friendship. Finding a mate and keeping the relationship going is a real challenge. You say the wrong things. You do the wrong things. Then before you know it, the once promising relationship is over. Engagement rings are given back and the wedding is called off.

People usually like a nice quiet life where everybody gets on and their moods are predictable. This is just not the case when a partner has bipolar. If your moods are unpredictable, relationships just dissolve. People get fed up and leave. They become like slippery eels sliding through your fingers.

The problem is when you are married your spouse will want attention, too, and if you are in a depressive episode, you will not have the energy to take care of yourself let alone anyone else. When depressed you will be self-absorbed and unable to take an interest in other people's problems.

This is difficult to understand for some people and makes the marriage very tricky. Most people think they can just say the magic word and you will get over your depression. They think you should snap out of it. You should go out and meet people and not be moping around the house all day. They may try to cajole you, but when that doesn't work, they get annoyed. They are only human after all, and we humans have only so much patience.

Then when you are manic, your poor partner will be utterly confused. Nothing they say seems to have any influence on you at all. You are up at three every morning sorting out closets and they can't understand what you are saying half the time because you are speaking so fast.

As you can see marriage and bipolar do not always go well together. The divorce rate is very high - 90% - so you need to consider carefully whether to get married or not. You should also discuss having children before you marry as bipolar is a genetic disease and can be passed on to your children.

I think the best thing to do is to be upfront with your partner early on. Maybe not on the first date because they might run a mile, but as the relationship progresses you need to try to explain your illness to them.

Some people are more receptive than others. They may even want to learn more about the illness and be very solicitous when you are ill. If this is the case with your partner, you may not have a problem. Hopefully, they will be able to forgive you when you say and do things that can be marriage breakers. Make sure you play your part by taking your medication religiously. If you are thinking of giving up taking your medications, the marriage may well fail.

Should I tell my daughter I have bipolar?

I wonder how old your daughter is and if she has been affected by your bipolar illness. Perhaps she is too young to assimilate the information. Even adults find it really difficult, if not impossible, to understand such a confusing illness as bipolar. I think most of this is because there is no cause or cure at the moment and people are confused when it comes to the workings of the brain and the mind.

I would only tell a young child if you are having bad depressions or manic episodes because it may help her to understand why Mommy is sick. You would have to find a way to explain it to her gently.

If your daughter is a teenager or an adult, I think you should divulge your illness. It may be difficult for you to explain it without the possibility of being judged, though. People are often quick to judge others and bipolar is not something you can help. You would have to explain that it is not something you have chosen for yourself. And you are doing things to stay well.

There is still a lot of stigma attached to mental illness, and bipolar in particular. People find it easier to talk about depression these days, but bipolar is often something people are very scared of. You might find it easier to tell her you have a mood disorder.

The other thing to bear in mind is that your daughter may well be frightened she will inherit it herself, and there is no doubt about it, bipolar is hereditary in some cases. That is not to say she will definitely be subject to bipolar, but there is a possibility. This could apply to any children she has as well.

If you do decide to tell her, it might be useful to give her something to read, something simple to understand would be best because bipolar is a very complex illness. Why not go online and find a concise explanation, then print it out and give it to her to read. When she has read it, you can discuss it with her if you choose to do so.

There is a magazine called BP that publishes a very concise explanation of Bipolar. You may enjoy the magazine yourself as they have some interesting articles.

Make sure you are doing everything in your power to keep your symptoms to a minimum. You will need to take your medication regularly, make sure you get adequate sleep and eat a nutritious diet. Hopefully, this will lessen your symptoms and your daughter will be able to see you are doing everything you can to stay well.

Why should I spend my life apologizing to people for things I said when manic?

What a wonderful question. Do I know the answer? No, I do not. I can tell you that only people with bipolar 1 have mania as people with bipolar 2 have hypomania which has the same symptoms but is not as serious as they are more in control of their world.

The problem is you can only be on one side or the other of this question, and it is impossible to know how the other person feels. Generally speaking, they just make a clean break and you have no idea what you said to upset them.

I have bipolar 1 which leaves me wide open to criticism when I am manic! You would really think I had committed a heinous crime the way many people have cut me off without explanation. It is very upsetting, but I haven't yet found the solution. I tend to stay away from people these days so there will be no trouble in the relationship.

I know I have offended people because they no longer talk to me, but I still don't know what I have said to them to cause a rift. Most of my family just avoided me when they got word of my illness. Even my sister could not, and would not, accept that I had bipolar and that some things were going to go awry with this illness.

Basically, most people do not want to hear your apologies or explanations. The only thing they care about is how much they have suffered at your hands. What they are suffering, I usually have to guess, but I do know that I didn't cause it on purpose. I have made numerous phone calls, written emails and long hand-written letters to many people, but so far have never been forgiven for my oversights. I must have said or done something really terrible, I just wish I knew what it was.

Occasionally, people do tell me what I have said, but it makes no sense. My ex-friend, who I loved dearly, now lives abroad and wrote to me for a couple of years. She writes very short letters, or rather emails, which tell you nothing at all about how she or anybody else is doing. It is just a lot of facts about where she has been and where she is going.

Once I wrote asking her to elaborate a bit, and she stopped writing altogether. Finally, when I managed to get hold of her on the phone, she said that as I did not want good news or bad news, she had no news at all for me. She said she could not cater to my illness and would not write to me again. If you can understand that way of thinking, you are more perceptive than me. I have no idea, to this day, what she meant by that response.

My one and only brother is different. He lives in Australia so doesn't have to put up with me much, but we do correspond quite frequently. I often wrote what he called my 'bipolar letters' and he didn't take them too seriously, but one time I wrote a particularly manic 'bipolar letter' by all accounts, and he found it very hard to forgive me for that. Needless to say, being a good brother, he did forgive me and we have carried on where we left off.

But I am always afraid that the other person will trigger me and I will do something I regret later. In a manic state, as you know, you are not aware of what is going on, and frequently say or do the wrong things.

How do you make your family understand your bipolar?

Everybody wants their family to understand them and what they are going through. If you were failing in school, or having problems with your husband, or even if you were depressed, they might want to hear about your situation. They might even try to help. But when it comes to bipolar disorder, things are different.

Nobody wants to know about bipolar disorder, especially families. The first thing that occurs to them is they might be responsible for your illness and it is all their fault. When someone feels that way there is usually nothing you can say that will change the situation.

Of course, bipolar is a genetic disorder, so it does have some relevance that you could have inherited it from someone in the family. When your bipolar diagnosis is out in the open, it is very tempting to look back and see where this illness began. Upon reflection, many people start to remember things their mother or their uncle said, or the strange moods their father has every now and then. Suddenly, it is a family affair, but they just don't want to admit it. Also, there is the fear that it might be passed on to the next generation.

Unfortunately, people often want to ignore bipolar. Sweep it under the rug. Pretend it is not happening. People are very resistant to things they do not understand and you cannot force them to listen to you. It is difficult enough for you to understand, I am sure, without trying to get your family members to understand it as well.

People who say they don't want to know are those who are afraid to talk about the illness. And many people are afraid of bipolar because it is a very confusing disease. And of course, stigma abounds and some family members will be afraid that the rest of the family or the neighbors will get to hear about it.

Many family members will likely turn their back on you and you will feel shunned. Personally, I would not divulge anything about my illness to anyone because nobody understands it, nor do they want to.

I can't keep relationships with anyone.
Am I the only one suffering from this?

I am sorry to say that it is considered "normal" for relationships to disappear down the toilet when you have this destructive illness. I know from bitter experience. So, you are not the only one at all. Most people with bipolar have this problem and don't know what to do about it.

The thing is people do not understand bipolar disorder. And most of the time, they don't want to, either. There is something they find very frightening about the illness, and they don't want to have anything to do with people who have it.

When you think about it, it is easy to understand why they find bipolar confusing. Bipolar makes us appear like three different people sometimes. Who they thought you were yesterday, is not who you are today. That happy, productive, creative person they were speaking to yesterday morning, is now an irritable, angry person who is crying all the time over nothing at all this afternoon. Then next week that same person is talking a mile a minute and rushing around spending money they don't have. They just don't understand bipolar. And who can blame them?

I wish I had some secret remedy for you, but I do not. I have lost most of my friends and relatives to bipolar and have never been able to make it up with them no matter how many times I have apologized for my erratic behavior.

Your only hope, seeing as it is very difficult to change yourself, is to change them. This means education. People are terrified of Bipolar - they are afraid they might catch it. They do not want to be around people who have this illness.

If you can possibly give them the information, they need to understand bipolar, you may well make inroads. You need all the support you can get. There are hundreds of books, articles, pod casts, blogs and You Tube videos out there. Also support groups for people with bipolar and for people who would like to support them.

Does a person with bipolar feel differently towards their partner depending on their mood?

That is a good question, but not an easy one to answer. Let me see what I can come up with.

Bipolar mood swings are depression and mania/hypomania. What this means is that a person who has bipolar has mood swings on top of what would normally be described as their personality.

They may usually have a bubbly personality, but would be very insular when they are depressed and feeling sad. On the other hand, a person who normally has a quiet, retiring personality, may be ecstatic and very loud when they are hypomanic. That is why people have a hard time understanding bipolar disorder, especially as it applies to their loved one.

When I experience a depressive mood swing, I never think about my partner, or anybody else for that matter. I am far too busy berating myself for all my supposed sins. I become very self-absorbed when depressed and can only think about all the terrible things I have done. I isolate and don't answer the phone. I don't want to talk to anybody.

My thoughts are along these lines:

"I just want to die".

Yes, that thought comes first, even before the first day of depression is over because I dive down into the pit so suddenly. This often applies when I have had a manic episode and depression has come the day after the mood subsides.

Next, thoughts:

"I must have done something terribly wrong to deserve this."

"I am totally worthless and am just taking up space in the world."

"My whole life has been one huge failure."

"I will never get over this depression. It will never get any better."

"Nobody likes me. They don't want to be bothered with me."

Then I spend a lot of my time imagining that I am sitting on the edge of a cliff in the middle of the night. The sky is black and the stars are pinpoints of light above me. The wind is blowing through my hair and I am shivering with the cold. I want to jump off the edge but am too tired to move. All I can think about is my death, and I want it to be over with quickly.

Now, would I think differently about the person I am with? I don't think so. I wouldn't think about them at all.

Then, let's think about mania and the wonderful mood I am in then. I can fly. I can do anything I want. I am Superwoman and everybody in this world should listen to what I have to say. I have so much energy I am cleaning out all the closets in my house, and while I am at it, I begin painting my kitchen cabinets.

I decide I really must get my novel finished so out comes the manuscript I started during my last mania, but no sooner do I start on that, I realize I really want to paint so out come all the oil paints. Then I think I shall read ten books at once and so on and so on. I spend a lot of time on the phone, even calling people up at two in the morning because I can't sleep.

Do you think I have a care in the world about anybody else and how they are feeling - I don't think so?

How do I explain to a man I like that I have bipolar?

It is always difficult to know whether to 'fess up' or not when it comes to sharing your story about bipolar. Sometimes it is a good thing, and sometimes a bad thing.

In your case, I would be reticent to talk about my bipolar to this person. If you were dating and about to get serious, then I would tell you, by all means, share that information. But as you say you only like this person, I would say be quiet.

If you were to tell him, it is almost certain that he would share this knowledge with others and this could cause you a lot of trouble.

Should you date him in the future and begin to get serious, I would tell him that you have a mood disorder and see how the conversation goes. If he is really interested and wants to know more about it, you could try printing out something about bipolar and giving it to him to read.

I think it is always wise to give out information slowly as many people are scared of bipolar disorder. There is still a great deal of stigma surrounding it.

I tend to keep that kind of information to myself if I can possibly help it. I have had some very bad experiences in the past and find it is not worth sharing.

PART FOUR
Depression

What happens when you get bipolar depression?

Depression is a progressive mood that is part of bipolar disorder. There is no demarcation line between being depressed and being severely depressed as depressive symptoms are on a continuum. Symptoms are not always linear either as depression can come and go, get worse, then get better only to get worse again.

Here is the story of Joe who has bipolar 2 and suffers from long depressive episodes:

One morning Joe woke up in a bad mood. He didn't want to get ready for work because he was feeling very tired. However, as he was in sales, he couldn't afford to miss a meeting with a client. He forced himself to take a shower, get dressed and go to work. The traffic was bad, and his day was filled with problems.

It was not like Joe to be irritable, but every little thing seemed to set him off. He drove to his client's office and lost his temper when someone cut him off. The client was a few minutes late, and Joe could barely contain his annoyance. The meeting went badly and he lost the sale.

Joe couldn't get to sleep at all the next night. He lay awake for hours thinking about the sale he had lost, and worrying that his boss would think his work was not up to par. Eventually, he did manage to sleep, but the next day he still felt tired and irritable. He made it to work, but everything he did took an extra effort.

Then Joe developed insomnia and hardly slept at all. This made him very irritable indeed. He also lost his appetite and his head began to feel as if it was stuffed with cotton wool. He had been Salesman of The Year, the year before, but now found he was unable to think clearly. He was afraid he might get fired.

Joe's mood became very gloomy indeed. He began thinking about how useless he was, and he wondered if he would ever be able to do his job properly again. He felt guilty for snapping at his wife. Nothing seemed to please him. He even got annoyed with the kids. His energy level was at an all-time low and he could barely drag himself across the room.

A few days later, Joe found that he couldn't stop crying. He had been brought up to believe that "big boys don't cry", so he felt extremely embarrassed and hid himself away in his bedroom watching TV most evenings. Whenever his wife came up to see how he was, he got very annoyed and told her to leave him alone.

Now Joe had a new symptom. He could not stop thinking about death. These thoughts kept going round and round in his head. He began thinking how he might kill himself. The problem was he didn't seem to have enough energy to make a plan.

After a few days, Joe found that he hardly had enough energy to take a shower. He just wanted to stay in bed all day and do nothing. Eventually, his wife persuaded him to call his boss and say he wouldn't be coming in.

Joe was unable to get out of bed at all now and felt like a little animal in hibernation. He lay all curled up in the fetal position and slept for hours. The whole day was spent sleeping and doing nothing else. Sometimes he slept for 16 hours straight. Even though he had always taken his medication regularly, it no longer seemed to be working. His wife told him she was very worried about him, and he would have to go into the hospital if he didn't improve.

At this point, Joe couldn't quite understand what was happening to him, but felt sure that he would never recover. The crying had stopped, but when he was awake his thoughts of death were intense. He found that he didn't mind the thought of dying. In fact, he thought it would be better for everybody if he was out of the way.

Joe had a distinct feeling that he was stuck at the bottom of a deep, dark well. The sides were made of mud and he realized there was no way to climb up the walls and get out. When he looked up all he could see was the black night sky above him. He didn't have the energy to try to climb out of the well so resigned himself to being left down there to die.

His wife finally called Joe's psychiatrist, and he was admitted to the hospital with severe bipolar depression.

What are some coping skills for depression?

We often hear about coping skills when it comes to bipolar depression - or bipolar in general - but not too many people apply these skills, or even know what they are. Coping skills do what they say, they help you cope, and this is all important when depressed.

You are quite likely to be holding down a job, or running a household, when you first start to feel depressed and it is useful to know what kind of things you could do to help yourself before the depression gets worse. Even if you are not working, and live alone, it is still important, maybe more so, that you have a plan to stay well.

Remember, it is best that you work on your Coping Skills BEFORE you get depressed.

It is no good trying to make a list when you are sick because your mind will not be able to wrap itself around the things you should be doing. Some of the first symptoms of depression are lack of concentration, being unable to focus, and being unable to think clearly. That is why you need to work on your plan the moment you notice a depressive mood swing coming on.

Making your plan.

Get out your journal, or a piece of paper will do fine to get you started. You can make it more elaborate later as you become better at developing your coping skills. When you are ready, be prepared to write down all the ideas you can possibly think of. It doesn't matter how silly they may seem, just keep writing until you run out of ideas. You can add to the ideas at any time in the future.

The important thing to remember is if you use your plan the moment you feel depression coming on you will more than likely get better.

Be aware of your symptoms whatever they may be. You may start to feel sad or guilty when you are getting depressed. You might even think you are worthless as a person. You may be thinking of death and suicide, or you may be crying. These are just symptoms of depression and can be helped with some appropriate coping skills.

Watch out for that little voice in your mind that tells you how stupid, ugly and useless you are. A negative voice in your mind is a very common symptom of depression. You may start thinking that people don't like you and you should stay out of everybody's way. Of course, we all know that isolation is bad for depression, but that is something you crave. You don't want to go out, you don't even want to answer the phone.

In order to help yourself, you need to be aware of your symptoms. You need to listen to that little voice inside your head and take action. This is what coping skills are all about.

Here are some of my coping skills to get you started on your own list:

- Take a couple of days off work.
- Rest or go to bed.
- Eat nutritious food and drink water regularly.
- Call or text a friend.
- Play some soft music and light some candles.
- Do some relaxation and visualization exercises.
- Look through photograph albums.
- Do some coloring.
- Sit outside in the sunshine.
- Go for a walk in the park.
- Do some gardening.
- Go for a drive.
- Do some journaling.
- Meditate.
- Draw or doodle.
- Do some Zen Tangles.

As you will see, I am not advocating that you get dressed and go out to dinner with your friends. The very last thing you want to do is to stay in the real world. Get off that merry-go-round for a while, take a nap, do whatever it takes to relax.

Now that you have read my list, it is time to make your own list of Coping Skills. Armed with your plan, you will be able to grab it whenever you start to feel depressed. Make sure you keep it in a prominent place where you can find it. It is very important to use your plan to prove to yourself that you are in control of your depression. When you are in control, you can and will get well.

What are the symptoms of depression?

The symptoms of depression are many and varied. They also differ from person to person. The main thing to remember when thinking about bipolar depression is that your symptoms are not you.

You as a person are totally separate from your symptoms. When you are well, you have your own personality, but when you are ill with depression your symptoms make you appear to be a different person altogether. Bipolar is like that. It is easy to lose track of the kind of person you are when you are well. It is easy to forget.

It is quite possible that you are the life and soul of the party when you are well – especially when you have bipolar hypomania or mania, yet, when you are sick with depression you can be silent, morose and irritable. This can really surprise some people, and quite often you are not treated as you would wish to be treated because you are frankly no fun to be around.

Here are a few of the symptoms of bipolar depression:

Extreme fatigue.

Feelings of sadness, guilt and worthlessness.

Irritability and anger.

Crying uncontrollably.

Loss of motivation to do the things you once enjoyed.

Wanting to be alone.

Not sleeping or sleeping too much.

Not eating or eating too much.

Not wanting to go out and meet people.

No energy to do the things you want to do.

Loss of libido.

Bodily aches and pains.

Thinking of death and suicide.

I have put thoughts of death and suicide at the end, although it is the most important symptom as it can easily lead to disaster. The thing to remember when you feel suicidal is that it is not a good way to end your suffering.

Suicide is a permanent solution to a tempory problem.

It is very important to tell someone if you feel suicidal. Most people will want to help you over this hurdle. If you have nobody to talk to, it is worth calling the number below:

National Suicide Prevention Lifeline: 1 800 273-8255

How can I explain to people what depression is like?

I am sorry you are feeling depressed. I can empathize with you because I have bipolar 1 and have experienced the same thing. I can't tell you how many times I have been unable to stay out of bed for more than an hour or so each day. It is bed to chair and chair to bed every day for weeks. Yet, I am sure other people think I am lazy, and should make more effort, but it is not possible to explain how you feel when you are deeply depressed if the person has never experienced it for themselves.

Nobody can know for sure what it feels like to be in another person's shoes. If you met a person who had terminal cancer, for example, you could not know what that feels like if you have never experienced it yourself. To be told you only have six months to live must be terrible, but if we are not given that death sentence ourselves there is no way of knowing how it would affect us. That's how it is with depression. You cannot expect people to understand how you feel.

Many people say they are depressed when what they really mean is that they are in a bad mood. All they know is that they feel miserable for a couple of days, but they don't realize the normal mood swings that people experience from day to day are nothing like the major shifts in mood experienced by somebody with bipolar disorder.

All you can hope for is that somebody understands that you have an illness which takes up all your energy. You can tell them that bipolar depression affects many bodily functions and causes your thoughts and activities to slow down considerably. Lying around on the couch all day is just part of a depressive episode. It has nothing to do with being lazy.

What is the worst thing you can do when you are depressed?

THE worst thing you can do when you are depressed is to kill yourself.

And many people do just that. Even more so if they have bipolar disorder. In fact, 1 in 5 people with bipolar do commit suicide, so the rate is far higher than the general population. And at least 50% of people with bipolar make suicide attempts, often several of them.

The problem is people do not take suicide threats seriously, yet nearly everybody who is about to commit suicide mentions their intentions to those closest to them. They are then told they don't mean it, or they are just trying to get attention. Then, suddenly, the person is dead.

It is essential for anybody who is suicidal to call the number below:

National Suicide Prevention Hotline: 1 800–273–8255

Even if you are only thinking about suicide and don't have a plan, it is a good idea to call the crisis hotline just to talk to somebody who understands. They have volunteers working 24/7 and they are accustomed to talking to people who are suffering from a broad spectrum of mental disorders.

Fortunately, a very depressed person does not often commit suicide because they are filled with inertia and lack of motivation. But when they begin to climb out of the depression and gain some strength, they may well make a serious attempt to end their lives.

If you are afraid of the urge to kill yourself, make sure you put away all dangerous things like knives, medications, and firearms. Call the Crisis Hotline and talk to them. If you are serious, and start to make a plan, do call 911 and find somebody to stay with you until the police arrive and take you to the hospital.

How do I stop feeling depressed? Should I try therapy?

I am glad you are feeling well enough to ask this question because that increases your chances of getting well. Many people do not realize they can change the course of their illness themselves, so they do not make the effort. Then, as time passes, it becomes increasingly difficult to alter your circumstances, and the depression only gets worse.

There are many ways to get well, but presuming you are on the right medications, a course in therapy may be the answer.

There are many different types of therapy to choose from: Behavioral Therapy; Trauma Therapy; Family Therapy; Gestalt Therapy; Cognitive Behavioral Therapy (CBT); Dialectical Behavioral Therapy (DBT); Talking Therapy, to name a few.

Research different therapies online, then ask the therapists in your area what type of therapy they do. Many therapists use facets of the skills they were taught in their training together with the experience they have gained from years of being in practice.

If you want to work on changing your negative thoughts, you could see a therapist for a 5 – 20 session course of CBT which has proved very successful for people with bipolar. The premise of CBT is that negative thoughts about an event or situation cause negative emotions and behavior. The event remains the same, but it is the way you interpret it that counts. So, identifying the event can help you see it in a more positive light. In turn, this will produce happier thoughts and emotions.

Sometimes, if you are disciplined, you can work on CBT on your own at home. Many people have been successful at this and you can get all the information you need online. This is a strategy you might find useful if you want to catch your depression in the early stages:

- Identify the event or situation that has upset you.

- What are your thoughts about this event or situation?

- What emotions are you experiencing because of these thoughts?

Now that you have progressed from EVENT to THOUGHT to EMOTION, you can ask yourself the following questions:

- Is the thought true?

- What evidence do I have?

- What are the chances that thought will happen?

- What's the worst that can happen?

- What would I do if it really happened?

What is a severe depressive episode like?

Bipolar depression comes in stages and gets worse the longer it lingers. If a person has been suffering from depression for a while and it becomes severe, they will be very ill indeed. Their symptoms may get so bad that they need hospitalization.

As anti-depressants take an average of two to three weeks to start working, the person may suffer even more than is necessary. That is why it is a good idea to see a psychiatrist and start a medication regime early in the depression when it has first taken hold.

Many people do not believe depression can get as bad as it does, on occasion. This is because they have never experienced it or know anybody who has. They think the person can will themselves out of it. Or they think they themselves are severely depressed but tend to describe symptoms of the early stages of depression, or even a bad mood they might be having for a few days. That is not severe depression.

These are some of the symptoms of severe depression:

Energy:

It is often too exhausting to walk across the room or even get out of bed when you are severely depressed. People often sleep for hours, sometimes 16 to 18 hours a day (hypersomnia). They just get out of bed to go to the bathroom, then fall back to sleep. The person in this state of despair will only improve with a great deal of help from a caring person.

Hygiene and personal care:

The thought of taking a shower is too much when you are severely depressed. Even brushing one's teeth can be difficult to accomplish because there is just no energy for anything. The worst thing is the person knows they need to do these things and feels very embarrassed and ashamed that they don't have the energy to do them.

Motivation:

The longer the depression lasts the less motivation the person has. Even eating and drinking are no longer appealing. Things that were once important when they were well are forgotten. The extent of the exhaustion will make it impossible to do anything at all.

Thoughts and Feelings:

The thoughts and feelings have now changed from guilt and sadness to hopelessness and helplessness. Many people say it feels like they should be able to force themselves to get out of bed, but cannot do so because all their strength has gone. Then, sadly, some people start feeling worthlessness as a person. They have done nothing wrong but feel as if they don't deserve to live.

Suicide:

By now thoughts of death and suicide are very strong. Psychic pain is excruciating and impossible to describe to others. It is important to get help at this stage before a life is lost to this illness.

5.7m adults in America have bipolar disorder.

Approximately 50% attempt suicide and 1 in 5 succeed.

What should I do to concentrate when I am depressed?

I am sorry to say, I think you are trying to do the impossible as it is incredibly difficult to concentrate when you are depressed. It is rather like me asking you, "How can I walk with a broken leg?" It cannot be done.

Loss of concentration is one of the major symptoms of depression, even in the early stages, and is something nobody likes to put up with. It makes us angry and frustrated, and it is difficult to achieve anything let alone get any work done. Information is going into your brain, but not getting processed quickly enough, if at all. Retaining and recalling the knowledge is even more difficult.

I give up reading when I am depressed. I can read a couple of paragraphs, then completely forget what I have read and must go right back to the beginning again. In the end, I have to accept I will not be able to concentrate properly until my depression has passed. It is rather like knowing you will not be able to walk again until your broken leg has healed.

Acceptance is always key to feeling better and less frustrated when depressed. It is sad to think we must accept depression, but sometimes there is no choice. When you have bipolar disorder, depression is just one pole of the illness, and not something we can often avoid.

One thing you can do is something that doesn't require concentration like coloring. There are many adult books for coloring, and it is so satisfying to work with all those beautiful colored pencils and create something you love. Or you can pass many hours doing Zen tangles. You might like to crochet or watch some old movies. Or you may prefer some outside activity like gardening or just kicking a ball around. Just whiling away the hours with nothing to tax the brain cells can be very good for depression.

Acceptance is key.

That will help your depression pass more quickly.

What are some things that can cause depression?

Many things can cause depression in bipolar. As you probably know, depression is lurking around the corner just waiting for an excuse to come out and ruin all the good things in your life.

I have bipolar 1 with more depression than mania, but many people have told me that depression affects people with bipolar 2 more deeply. Either way, many people with bipolar often say they hardly get a break from depression at all. Interestingly, bipolar 1 disorder, with full-blown mania, does not need a history of depressive episodes to make a diagnosis.

Here are a few things that can cause depressive episodes in Bipolar Disorder:

Loss

If a person experiences adverse events like a loss of some kind, it is a normal part of the grieving process to feel depressed for a period of time. It is when it doesn't go away, or gets worse, that intervention is needed, often in the form of anti-depressant medications. Yet some people with bipolar will not experience an episode of depression at all, even though it seems as if they have plenty to be depressed about.

Stress

There is no doubt that stress can cause depression in bipolar. We live in a stressful age and there is plenty of stress to go round. The causes of stress are innumerable: You may have lost your job, and not have enough money to live on, or you may discover you have a fatal illness. These, and many other examples, are cause for alarm and they can easily lead to depression in bipolar.

Stress brings out a sense of helplessness in the face of adversity. No matter which way you turn, there is no solution to be found. Then, of course, the fear involved in what will happen in the future causes anxiety and panic which only exacerbates the situation further. Stress can be very damaging to your health and can precipitate a mood swing.

Mood cycles

Bipolar depression is not necessarily a reaction to things going wrong in your life. Depressive mood cycles come and go in bipolar. Half the time you never know when they will hit and cannot control them.

Things can be going along quite smoothly, then you are blindsided by yet another depressive episode. It is this that makes bipolar such a difficult illness to live with. One day you may be fine, then the next day you may wake up in a deep depressive mood and all has changed in your world. It is this uncertainty that causes so much fear in bipolar.

Some people cycle at certain times of the year, and they know that come spring or fall depression will appear despite their best efforts. This can also be diagnosed as SAD (Seasonal Affective Disorder) in some people.

Post mania

Bipolar depression can also be brought about by a sudden drop in mania/hypomania. You could have been on top of the world for a period, then suddenly you crash into depression. It is often true to say, "The higher you go the lower you fall."

Many other things can cause bipolar depression - there are too many to list here – but it is highly likely that you have experienced them yourself at some point in your life.

Of course, there is the added problem of taking anti-depressants with bipolar disorder as some (particularly the SSRIs) can cause a rebound manic/hypomanic episode. Anti-depressants must be prescribed with caution for that very reason.

If you want to be able to control your depression to some extent, you could try doing bipolar mood charts. At least you may have an idea of when you will crash, then you can be prepared to take better care of yourself for a few days. You can find dozens of mood charts online, on an app, or make them yourself. Unfortunately, ready-made mood charts don't always cover your form of bipolar. I had mixed episodes for a long time and had to make my own chart to cover everything.

How do you deal with depression when your family and friends won't help you?

It is sad, but your family and friends are not a good support system for you. These people have demonstrated to you that they do not want that responsibility. Unfortunately, that is the truth, so you need to stop relying on them for help. When you are depressed, you need people who have sympathy/empathy and your family and friends have proved to you that they do not.

People have many different reasons for being unavailable when it comes to depression, or indeed bipolar. They may think you are bluffing because you are usually strong, but it is more likely that they are frightened of becoming depressed themselves as if depression is a contagious disease. Or quite possibly, they just don't care. People like this will never understand something they have never experienced so it is a waste of time trying to enlist their help.

I have found this to be a delicate problem. My relatives and friends all ran a mile when they heard about my bipolar illness. My one brother has stood by me, but even he has little interest in learning about bipolar and is unable to help me when I am suffering from a depressive episode no matter how hard he tries. The fact that he lives 10,000 miles away doesn't help either!

I would say, it is best for you to ignore these people and find help elsewhere. That is much easier said than done, I know. It takes a bit of planning, but with determination, you can build a good support system for yourself.

I would think of your psychiatrist as the first person on your list of supporters. Hopefully, you are taking medication for your depression, so your doctor will understand your situation better than most people.

If you are fortunate enough to have a psychotherapist or councilor, they would be number two on your list of supporters. By going to therapy you will be able to talk about your everyday problems, and the therapist should be able to help you cope. His support can be invaluable to your well-being.

If there is a clinic near you, I would take advantage of that. I know not everyone is fortunate enough to have a mental health clinic in the same town, but even if you need to travel it might be well worth a visit. I go to a clinic quite regularly and I have a case worker who is very helpful in developing my goals, and I have a Peer Group Worker who comes to my house every two weeks to discuss my progress.

Don't forget peer support groups. You may have one near you that you can visit. NAMI (National Alliance on Mental Illness) are in most towns, and they can be very helpful. You can build your support system there and learn more about your illness from their frequent lectures.

There are also many online Support Groups where you can post questions or give answers to other people from around the world. They usually have a private message board as well, so you will be able to make friends with people who have the same disorder as you.

Be resourceful. Look around you and think in terms of people being helpful towards you. It is surprising who will help even when you hadn't thought about them before. I find that my dentist is very knowledgeable about bipolar disorder and helps me through dental treatment if I am depressed. He also takes an interest in my medications which is essential in dentistry.

It can be very difficult to build a support group, I know, but you might need to look in the unlikeliest of places. I used to see my bank manager for help balancing my check book when I first came out of the hospital, and you would think she would be the unlikeliest person to help me. But she has a relative who has bipolar, so she is able to understand the problems I have with money. She keeps an eye on my account in case my spending gets out of hand during episodes of mania.

So, never give up. There are people out there willing to help. Just don't expect your family or friends to volunteer their services.

How do I cope with loss of motivation?

If you have depression, you know what it means to lose your motivation, even for things you once enjoyed. It is a cruel trick that depression plays on us, and no fault of our own. This is particularly true of artistic interests as depression seems to interfere with the creative process.

It is sad when a person can no longer paint or play sports, but even worse when their job entails being creative and productive every day. It would be difficult playing in an orchestra or appearing on stage when you are depressed. And if you work in advertising or marketing, where you must come up with a steady stream of ideas, it is hard to keep your job. Depression is a thief in the night. Along with snatching your confidence, it robs you of all your motivation.

When I am depressed, I know all about this loss of motivation. I just sit in a chair and look straight ahead with nothing registering at all. I am in no fit state to attempt to do anything, I just don't have the interest.

Usually, I am a very busy person and have many creative interests like drawing, painting and writing. However, when depression takes hold, I am no longer able to do any of these things because I lose interest in everything. Some days, it is enough to take a shower and brush my teeth. When I am depressed, I can no longer find the motivation or energy for housework or cooking either.

I imagine your depression looks something like mine. If this is the case, why would you keep beating yourself up? You know it is not your fault. It is the depression talking. You need to seriously consider being kind to yourself and stop putting yourself through such a guilt trip. If it was somebody else, you probably would not blame them because you could easily see how depressed they were. You would not want to keep pushing them to do things when they are not motivated to do them.

As one psychiatrist told me, just do one thing a day when you are depressed. Put a load of laundry in the washing machine, then sit down and rest. Take it out of the washing machine the next day and put it in the drier. If you can put it away when it is dry, all well and good, but if not, you will need to make it a three-day endeavor. The main thing is to do something small and be proud of your accomplishment.

There will always be people who have no understanding of depression. They cannot possibly know what it means to be so ill you just don't have the energy to walk round the block. Forgive their ignorance. Forgive yourself. Realize you are sick and stop pushing yourself. If you had the flu you would go to bed and not do anything for several days. Nobody would blame you because they have had the flu and remember how bad they felt.

Just be kind to yourself. Let yourself off the hook. It is an illness you didn't ask for; it just chose you. Let other people go their own way and do things for you if they can. Spend what little energy you do have on getting well.

How should depressed people make major decisions?

Unfortunately, depression affects a person's decision-making ability leaving them unable to think clearly. It's as if a cloud comes down and encompasses the brain. Many people call this, 'Brain Fog.' People who are depressed often suffer from brain fog and agonize over every decision that must be made. It's like their thoughts are in turmoil, spinning round in their head, and there is nothing to stop them. Nothing makes sense any longer.

And worse, depressed people tend to think negatively about everything - they expect things to go wrong all the time. With this attitude, things often do go wrong, and they are not disappointed. They also lose their confidence, and this causes them to think that any decision they make will be the wrong one, and they will live to regret it.

Even simple decisions become difficult when you suffer from depression. Just going to the supermarket can be daunting. You walk around the store in a daze and are suddenly faced with one hundred different types of cereal on the cereal aisle. And if you should visit the deli, you will not only have to choose which type of ham you would like, but also how you would like it sliced. Is it better to have thick or thin slices? You don't know. You just want ham. It is nice to have choices when you are well, but when you are feeling sick you just want to pick something, anything, or have somebody else pick it for you.

The best thing to do when shopping is to make a list and stick to it. That way you will come home with what you need rather than a lot of luxuries you really have no use for and may even break the budget. Some people carry a calculator and keep a running tally as they shop. This can be very useful when depressed because it prevents you from filling up your cart with items you may never use. There is no doubt about it, shopping is difficult when you are depressed, so make it easy on yourself.

But what if you must make a major decision? For example, you may need to decide on whether to go to a wedding. Or maybe, you are called upon to choose a new appliance when an old one breaks down. Or you could possibly have to decide on something even more important and be completely at a loss as to what to choose.

Get help. Go to your doctor, your school principal, your bank manager, your minister, or your lawyer. Many people will be able to help you make an important decision. If all else fails, ask somebody you trust like a family member or a good friend. It is best not to rely on your decision-making abilities when you are feeling depressed.

It is the same when you experience a major loss of some kind. People will always tell you not to make any life-changing decisions for at least a year. Major decisions like moving to another house can prove to be huge mistakes down the road, and abruptly leaving a job can amount to all kinds of problems. Of course, ideally, it is best to leave major decisions until you start to feel well again. Forgive yourself for your indecisiveness and wait until the depression has passed.

How horrible is depression?

Depression is a devastating illness that changes who you are. It is horrible. It is always horrible. Anybody who tells you otherwise is lying. Depression is always horrible for one reason, and I will tell you what that is:

When you are depressed, you start to lose hope of ever getting well again. And we all need hope to cling to.

Depression is a progressive illness. It starts out with feeling tired and maybe a little irritable, but soon progresses into feelings of sadness and hopelessness. Your head feels like it is full of cotton wool, and you can no longer do the things you used to take for granted.

You slowly begin to realize that you are not fit for this world, and start to think you'll never get better. You get desperate. It feels like drowning. You would kick and scream if you had the energy. But you don't.

Soon enough, you start to feel like a failure. You are so tired you cannot do the things you used to do, including doing your job and looking after your family. And, if you would admit it to yourself, you no longer want to live. In fact, all you can think about now is death and dying. You think you would be doing your family a favor if you killed yourself, but you just don't have the energy to make a plan.

Now hopelessness is really setting in.

You find you have no energy to take a shower, and no desire to take a shower either. People try to help, but you know in your heart that nothing can help you. You might as well give up.

You lose hope of ever getting well again.

I have felt like this many times. I have been through the sadness, the tiredness, the loss of motivation. I have laid for days on end in my bed.

When I finally lost hope, I just wanted to die. That is how horrible depression really is.

What triggers depressive mood swings?

Triggers are very personal. What makes me depressed might have no appreciative effect on you whatsoever, and vice versa. Take clothes, for instance. If you love blue you wear blue a lot of the time and you rarely wear black because you know it will make you feel depressed. Whereas I might hate wearing blue clothes, so my wardrobe is filled with black dresses and sweaters. Black makes me feel relaxed.

With mood swings, you must choose your triggers wisely and not indulge in the things you know will make you suffer unnecessarily.

The best way I know of doing this is to make a list. Don't rush into it. Make your list slowly as you discover what causes you to feel depressed. It may take you a month or more to complete your list, but that is fine because you will be well-armed when a trigger pops up in your life.

On the other hand, don't be a slave to your list. What triggers you one day, may not trigger you at all the next time you come across it. In fact, the more you are aware of what triggers your depression, the more likely you are to conquer it.

For example, I always used to be triggered by hunger which caused a dip in my mood. I have a very bad habit of forgetting to eat when I am busy. And I am always busy. I spend hours and hours on writing or artwork and rarely stop to eat. I can honestly say, I don't even feel slightly hungry. The time just passes, and I forget to eat. Then suddenly, I realize I am hungry because my stomach is growling, and I find that I don't have the energy to fix something. Now that I know this is one of my triggers, I can prepare myself by making something early in the day so that I can stop what I am doing for fifteen minutes and eat it. No more hunger and no more mood swings.

You may find that you are triggered by certain toxic people - family, friends, colleagues - it doesn't matter who. These people are so detrimental to your health that you always start feeling sick when you are with them. Sometimes, it is hard to avoid them, but once you know you shouldn't be entertaining them so much in your life it is often easier to limit your contact with them.

The same goes for environments. If a place puts you in a bad mood, don't go there unless you really must. If you are miserable in your job, don't waste time there feeling bad, move on and find work that you enjoy doing. As you know, work and bipolar sometimes don't mix because what you are doing is too taxing. In that case, it may be wise to work part-time, or find other work that is more conducive to your mental health.

You can make a list if you feel it would help you. You can include things that have a detrimental effect on your mood - maybe staying up too late, drinking too much alcohol, or any other activity you engage in which until now you hadn't recognized was your downfall. Make your list judiciously. Avoid what you can, or if you really can't avoid it entirely, limit your exposure to it.

Is being overwhelmed a symptom of depression?

Well, it could be a symptom of depression, although it is not listed as one, but I think it is much more likely to relate to anxiety which often comes with bipolar, or panic, or plain old stress. To say that it doesn't occur in depression would be false, though, because when depressed our thoughts are not clear, and the loss of motivation often means that things pile up around us and everything needs to be tackled at once.

Being overwhelmed is a terrible feeling, no matter what the cause, and it is often difficult to recover from. The feelings of being overwhelmed can sometimes lead to doing nothing for days or weeks at a time, and this makes the depression even worse. Hoarding is a good example of being overwhelmed, and the complications that can arise.

I know how it feels to be overwhelmed and unable to cope with everyday life. Everything runs away with me, and I get so frantic with all the demands that are being imposed on me I ring my friend in tears.

I usually stand and stare at the scattered papers on my desk and sigh with dismay. How on earth is one person supposed to cope with all these things on their own, I ask myself? And everything has a deadline which makes matters worse. Each piece of paper must be dealt with this minute, it seems, and none of that is possible when I am in this strange mood. I just want to opt out of life altogether until the horrible demands are gone.

But, of course, these demands do not pass on their own. All my scheduled appointments must be attended to, and those horrible mounds of paperwork will need to be sorted out soon because nobody else is likely to walk in and help me do it.

And what about all the phone calls I must make? I have lists of phone calls that go on for days because, no matter how many times you leave messages, people never call you back. I have found in life that people will only call you if they want something. Otherwise, if you want something, you must keep bugging them.

I think being overwhelmed is the result of the 21st Century rat race. How anybody copes is a miracle. It just takes one more thing to push them over the edge. If you have somebody else available to help you sort through the chaos, you are very lucky indeed.

The cure for this situation is to make an orderly stack of papers on the desk, go through them one at a time, and write on them: CALL, WRITE, FILE. Then divide the stack up again into these sections and prioritize. Do the things that are urgent right there and then and leave the non-urgent things for another day. You can even plot out the items in your schedule book so you won't forget to do them. Crossing them off will give you a sense of satisfaction. Don't forget to give yourself a big pat on the back and a nice bowl of chocolate ice cream when you are finished.

How can someone help you when you are depressed?

The strange thing is, the more serious your depression, the less likely it is that anyone can help you. That is why it is best to talk to your loved ones when you first become depressed, before you sink any further. If, for example, you tell them you are having a problem with going in to work or looking after the kids, they may be able to reassure you and will be there to help you, if that is at all possible.

Of course, with bipolar, not all things are possible when it comes to a support system. I am acutely aware of this myself as I have a very shaky support system. Most of my friends and relatives have long since departed.

However, if people do want to help, you can tell them you don't have the energy to do what you used to do, and they will need to be patient with you for a while. Most people will understand and, hopefully, will help you with the housework or looking after the kids until you begin to feel better.

Be sure to take your medication as prescribed by your doctor as this will help enormously. Remember, though, that it can take two to three weeks to work. At least you will be taking a step forward and your loved one will see that you are trying.

You may find that you feel very guilty because you are depressed - it comes with the territory, along with sadness and feelings of worthlessness. Being unable to work, or unable to fulfil your role in the household can be very upsetting. On the other hand, there doesn't need to be any reason for the guilt. Bipolar depression can just happen.

You will have very little energy because depression is draining. It is not a case of not wanting to do things. You just don't have the energy to do them. If someone is trying to force you to do the things you usually do when you are well this can be extremely burdensome. You need to make it clear that you need to rest. Rest is good for depression. It lessens the chance of the depression getting worse.

If your depression does get worse, and you sink into defeat, it becomes difficult to talk to others at all, and they will feel useless and have no idea how to help you. They will see you are no longer motivated and have lost interest in everything. This can be disturbing for someone who cares about you, so you can try to explain to them that you don't have the energy to do anything right now.

Should the depression worsen, and you are unable to get out of bed, your loved ones will probably feel guilty or impatient. They may be able to encourage you to get up and take a shower, but even this may be difficult for you.

I have often been severely depressed and putting the toothpaste on the toothbrush was too much for me. Besides when you are that depressed, you cannot understand what needs to be done because your mind will not work properly and you will be confused.

It is good that people want to help, and you need to be grateful for that. Try to understand it is difficult to sit back and watch a person deteriorate. If things do not resolve themselves, the only thing they can do at this stage is to call the doctor who may admit you to the hospital. We hope it never comes to this, but when severe depression takes over, it is the safest place to be.

What is your unpopular opinion about depression?

Since I have bipolar disorder, I am no stranger to depression and have had more episodes of depression in the past than I can possibly remember. Like most people with bipolar depression, I have taken every medication known to man, spent many hours crying in psychiatrists' offices, had years of therapy, and forced myself to get out and do all the things that we are told to do. All to no avail.

I still take medication because I would be a real fool to stop doing that. I still see my psychotherapist twice a month because he is my rock and always there for me. However, I am finally taking my therapist's advice and recovering from my depressive episodes in a few days instead of weeks.

The secret to this is to stop the fight.

People always think you should be out there with your boxing gloves on, fighting the good fight, forcing yourself to do all manner of things you feel much too ill to do. That will not shorten your depression, more than likely it will make it worse.

The answer is to go with the flow.

Yes, accept that you are depressed and it will pass, just like it always has. Think of it like the sea. You are floating on the sea and the choppy waves are churning all around you, but if you don't struggle you can easily keep afloat, and you will eventually find the shore.

But if you are out at sea panicking, kicking your legs about, getting breathless, and battling with the waves, you will drown.

The key is acceptance.

* Say to yourself, "I am depressed."

* "I accept the fact that I don't feel well, so I am not going to push myself to do things."

* "I am just going to relax until this passes." And it will.

I realize you have been fighting the good fight for years, and it is very difficult to just give up and rest. But if you are able to do this, you will find that you feel much better in a couple of days, before you get so bad you can't get out of bed.

At first you will have all the symptoms of depression:

- Feeling sad, worthless and guilty.

- No energy to cook a meal.

- No motivation to do the things you like to do.

- Negative and pessimistic thoughts.

- Constant thoughts of death and dying.

These things are just symptoms of depression. They are not you. You are just fine, but at the present time you are experiencing the very unpleasant symptoms of depression. Even suicidal thoughts are quite normal. They are just another symptom of depression. If you don't act on them, you will be fine.

Next time you feel depression coming on, be kind to yourself. If you had the flu, you would feel so bad you would have to give in to it and rest. Well, that is what you can do with depression. Remember to eat properly and do some light exercise if you are up to it. You would do well to sit outside in the sunshine, too. As always, drink plenty of water so that you don't become dehydrated, then soon you will start to feel better. The guilt of not doing things is very difficult to overcome, I know. But remember:

We are human beings not human doings

I hope you will try this simple method some time when you are at the very beginning of a depressive episode before it has taken hold. You will then see how quickly you begin to feel back to your usual happy self.

Is atypical depression related to bipolar?

Yes, atypical depression is related to bipolar and major depressive disorder. Oddly enough, I had no idea what atypical depression was until recently. Now I see this is what I have suffered from for many years without realizing it.

Unfortunately, I have been reluctant to discuss this with the medical profession because it is not like unipolar depression or even bipolar depression in many ways. I didn't want them to question me about it because they might think I had made it up, and I wasn't really depressed at all. In short, I felt guilty.

Here is an example of atypical depression:

Say you were depressed, and someone invited you out for dinner one night. It would seem impossible to go out in the face of how depressed you have felt for a while, however, when you do manage to get dressed and go out, you find you have a pretty good time. Then, sadly, the depression returns just as badly the next day.

You can temporarily brighten up in a doctor's office and tell the doctor there's nothing wrong with you, only to find some hours later you are back where you started. I have been in the hospital and told a psychiatrist I wasn't depressed. He said, "What are you doing here, then?" which was a perfectly reasonable question.

Atypical depression is confusing. It seems very unfair that you can climb out of the depression, but it is only temporary. It also makes you feel guilty having to explain to people that you felt better yesterday but feel ill again today.

There are many symptoms of atypical depression. Here are a few:

- You can brighten up when something positive happens, only to revert back to the depressed state again within hours or days.

- Binge eating.

- Hypersomnia (sleeping for long periods, even 16 - 18 hours a day.)

- Anxiety and panic attacks.

- Lethargy where the limbs feel very heavy.

People with atypical depression often have personality disorders, like borderline, and have the following problems on top of those listed above:

- Impulsive behaviors.

- Easily angered.

- Envy.

- Give up on goals very easily.

- Tend to under-achieve.

- Fixate on past shameful or embarrassing experiences.

- Self-harm.

- Feelings of emptiness and boredom.

- Mood swings.

- Intense fear of rejection.

- Unstable self-image.

They also make increased suicidal attempts, have weight gain, and often use alcohol or illegal substances to self-medicate.

If you think you are suffering from atypical depression, I advise you to see a doctor right away as treatment is available. People with this disorder often respond well when anti-depressant medications are added to their other medications. I am taking two anti-depressants these days and feeling fine.

Why do I feel worthless when I am depressed?

Thinking you are worthless makes you feel sad. You think you have no value as a human being. This thought is a judgement and causes low self-esteem. We tend to judge ourselves mercilessly when we are depressed.

Depression

Depression itself can cause feelings of worthlessness since it is one of the major symptoms. We may feel empty and useless, and no amount of persuasion by others can shake this belief. It is very painful to think you have no value on this earth. It makes living seem pointless and is one of the causes of suicidal ideation.

Circumstances

Circumstances can cause a person to feel worthless, especially when a loss of one kind or another has occurred. There may have been a rejection of some kind - a job loss, a breakup, a divorce, a criticism, burn out, or even the death of someone which can result in feelings of abandonment. It is easy for the person to think if someone they love has died it is because they didn't think they were worth living for. Circumstances can bring about bipolar depression quite often.

Long standing feelings of shame

Feelings of worthlessness often cause shame. Then shame pervades everything the person thinks about or does in life. It can cause long-term embarrassment and can be exacerbated if the person has bipolar disorder.

When we look at depression, in particular bipolar depression, we can often see that this feeling of worthlessness goes with the territory. Bipolar depressions are usually short lived, so you are not consumed by this feeling for a long time. It is devastating to feel worthless as a person. It influences everything you do. If those feelings are intense, it can extend the depression for some time.

When you feel worthless because of a loss of some kind that can easily lead to depression. This means the depression you experience in bipolar can be brought on by your circumstances at the time. That is the nature of bipolar depression. It may have an identifiable cause, or not.

Long-standing feelings of worthlessness generally have their roots in childhood. If you suffered abuse or neglect when you were young, it is quite possible that feelings of shame will ensue. Shame is not like guilt. When you feel guilty it is because you have done something wrong. You know it is not about you, but about the act.

When you feel long-standing shame, it is because you think there is something wrong with you as a person which is a very difficult feeling to overcome. This can lead to long-term depression if you have bipolar or not. If this is the case, I would advise you to go to therapy so you can face the situation and learn to accept that you have value in life.

How do you tell the difference between boredom and depression?

Boredom is a state of being, it is not an illness. If you find something that interests you then your boredom will likely decrease. It is not a permanent condition, nor harmful.

People say they are bored all the time, yet there is so much to do these days that I find it hard to believe. Even a couple of hours on the internet can solve the problem because there is so much to learn and enjoy. It is always good to have an inquiring mind. Curiosity is what helps us progress in life and be creative.

Why not learn a foreign language or brush up your math skills? And if you use *YouTube* you can find something new to do every day. The possibilities are endless when using the internet, but there are many other ways to reduce boredom. You could join a club where you can meet people with your interests. You could also learn how to play a musical instrument or appear in a play.

Depression is an illness. It affects the way you think and function in your everyday life. Most of all it affects how you feel about yourself. For example, your mood changes to that of sadness, guilt or worthlessness, and you think a lot about death and dying all the time. With these negative thoughts comes a loss of desire to do anything you used to like doing.

Quite often you want to just sit and stare at the wall, or cry. Even taking a shower or brushing your teeth takes too much effort. Some people sleep a lot, even 16 hours a day is not at all unusual when you are depressed. And some people become so depressed that they are unable to get out of bed at all except to use the bathroom.

Depression is all consuming and lasts for extended periods of time, whereas boredom can usually be fixed immediately if you put your mind to it.

What is the hardest thing to face when you are depressed?

When you first become depressed, I tend to think the hardest thing to face is the eternal lack of energy to the point of exhaustion. Even when sitting down, the exhaustion overcomes you. You try to fight the depression, but it doesn't work, so you end up going from bed to chair, chair to bed for hours. And the time passes slowly.

People with depression have a very limited amount of energy, so you must forgive yourself if you are unable to accomplish much during the day. Bipolar affects a person's thinking, feeling, behavior and energy. So, it is natural to want to lie around doing nothing.

I think it is very common to feel as if you are being lazy when you are depressed, but it is difficult to communicate how you feel to others. There are many insensitive people who will not be able to understand this at all. They like to think of people as always being productive, but depression doesn't allow for productivity, or creativity either, because you inevitably lose interest in everything.

When you start to get depressed, you can feel yourself walking more slowly across the room, but there is no way you can walk faster because your legs feel so heavy. And when in severe depression, it is not unusual to go to bed and sleep for hours on end. Anyone who has had severe bipolar depression will no doubt be able to identify with this lack of energy as it is a universal feeling.

Then oddly, when in mania the opposite is true. You have so much energy you can be up at 3 o'clock in the morning cleaning house and sorting out cupboards without getting tired at all. The wonderful feeling rushes through your veins making you wonder how on earth you had so little energy only last week when you were depressed.

So, forgive yourself for your loss of energy. This too shall pass.

Is there a way of coping with the sadness of bipolar depression without medications?

It is a well-known fact that bipolar disorder cannot be managed successfully without medication. Many people claim otherwise, but they often succumb to the illness and end up in the hospital.

There is no known cure for bipolar, but fortunately it can be treated with medication, therapy and a change in life-style which makes most people's lives more manageable.

To suggest that you can cope with the sadness of depression without medication is like saying you can control your high blood pressure without anti-hypertensives. It simply cannot be done. That is the reason why these medications, especially mood stabilizers, are successful in treating the varying mood swings in bipolar disorder.

There is no saying that the medications are a guarantee, or without side effects, as no medication is fool proof, but your chances of remaining well on medication is infinitely greater than without it.

As with most people, you must be patient and diligent in finding the right medication for you. Pharmacology is an art and a science, and it can take many different cocktails before finding the right one for you. It is very difficult to treat bipolar disorder as the doctor is dealing with two separate moods swings and you are a unique individual.

I have tried about thirty different cocktails over my life time, as medicines often stop working over a period of time, but I have now found something that works for me. Side effects can be a big problem with all medications, but there are an infinite number of medications that can be tried before giving up.

You will rarely be symptom-free, even with medication, as bipolar has a sneaky way of creeping up on you, but to try to struggle with depression without medication is an uphill battle.

There are many things you can try to help your symptoms once you have found a medication that gives you some relief. I hope you are in therapy as this is known to be necessary to help with everyday problems in bipolar. And I also hope that you are vigilant about your life-style. You cannot do all the things you used to do without causing problems with the illness.

Nobody likes living with bipolar, but when help is available, we must take it. That is the only way we are to live a near normal life.

PART FIVE
Mania and hypomania

How do manic attacks happen?

Unfortunately, there doesn't seem to be any rhyme or reason behind a bipolar manic episode, except to say you are clinically cycling. This is obviously not something you are aware of, though. Mania usually occurs without any warning so there is no time to prepare, and no chance of stopping it. In fact, it is a real challenge to be able to make a difference before mania really sets In.

One thing that can lead to mania is lack of sleep - only getting three or four hours sleep for two or three nights in a row. This leaves the door wide open for mania. That is why your lifestyle counts so much in bipolar disorder, and nobody can fix this for you.

If you are the type of person who likes to party, and spends most nights out drinking until 3 in the morning, you are literally asking for a manic episode. After a few episodes like this, it is usually easy for people to cut back on the late nights and drinking which only interfere with the medications anyway.

If I miss one night of sleep, I start to feel myself getting all jangly the next day. I am always careful to take a nap in the afternoon if I possibly can. Just lying quietly under the covers helps, too. Of course, in the lead up to mania, the very last thing you want to do is lie quietly, but it is really advised if you want to avoid a manic episode. Do keep a sleep aid next to the bed in case you need it.

There are a few signs that you might watch for before mania:

- You may start having more exciting ideas, and your thoughts start to speed up.

- Sometimes people start to enjoy loud music and colorful clothes.

- Others suddenly start sabotaging relationships which they sorely regret later.

The problem is, when you are heading for a manic episode, it is easy to think you are very well and certainly not sick, which makes it more difficult for others to intervene. If you can possibly spot it yourself and go to the psychiatrist, he will make sure that you are taking the right medications. Do not start thinking you are so well that you don't need medication, either.

Unfortunately, once mania has set in, there is often no stopping it and you must ride it out. If it is bad you may end up in the hospital, or at the very least need a higher dose of medication.

If you have a lot of manic episodes, you might be able to notice some pattern which is occurring. If you can write this down in a diary and remember to look at it when your mood starts changing, you just may be able to stop the mania by taking things easy for a few days. It would be ideal if you had a partner who understood this pattern so that they can help you stop the mania before it gets bad.

It might be a good idea to make an arrangement with your partner before you actually get manic. You can write down a few things that they could do to help you. Here are a few that come to mind:

1. Take your phone and credit cards away.

2. Remove weapons and knives.

3. Listen to your story without challenging your beliefs.

4. Ensure you that they can be there with you.

5. Tell them not to physically grab you or yell at you because it only escalates the mania and can make you more paranoid and violent.

6. Use a signal to help them realize you feel unsafe.

7. Take you to the hospital if you or others are in danger.

If you would like to try mood charts, that is another way you can keep track of the days leading up to mania, especially if they are a regular occurrence. You can find many different types of mood charts on the internet or make your own.

Do you need to have bipolar to experience mania, or can anyone have these symptoms?

Only people with bipolar 1 disorder experience true mania. It can be confusing because many people say, 'Oh, he is manic," when what they really mean is that he is happy for a few days. Maybe he just bought a new device, or even a new car. In these circumstances it is natural to be happy, but that is not bipolar 1 mania.

The difference between bipolar episodes and the normal ups and downs of everyday life that most people experience is the severity of the symptoms. In order to be diagnosed with bipolar 1 you would need to experience vastly exaggerated manic symptoms.

The symptoms of mania are as follows:

1. Feeling ecstatic about life
   - a total reversal of the loss of energy experienced in depression.

2. Feeling omnipotent and far superior to the average person.

3. Unable to sleep, or needing very little sleep, yet still able to function well.

4. Being very productive and creative.

5. Having many projects on the go at once, but trouble finishing them.

6. Being entertaining but having such rapid thoughts and speech patterns that people become uncomfortable in your presence.

7. Feeling angry and having episodes of rage.

8. Taking risks like vastly over-spending, speeding, opening businesses that fail later, and having promiscuous, unprotected sexual encounters with strangers.

Mania and hypomania (as experienced by people with bipolar 2) have similar symptoms. But the person with mania will have wildly exaggerated symptoms and be totally out of control. The only course of treatment left at this time is usually a hospital admission. People with hypomania (as seen in bipolar 2) rarely go into the hospital. Their hypomania can usually be controlled by a change in medication or a change in the dosage of the old one.

There are many more symptoms if you wish to study bipolar on the Internet, but those will give you a general idea. If you are one of the many millions of people who just experience life's ups and downs, there is nothing to worry about.

How do you transition from hypomania to mania?

This is a very difficult question to answer because there is no demarcation line when it comes to the transition from hypomania into mania. It is a process and comes on gradually in most cases. I have bipolar 1 and have had more hypomanic and manic episodes than I would like. In fact, I have had a whole lifetime of them.

What is different about hypomania and mania is that you are generally aware of what is happening while you are experiencing hypomania, but your awareness does a nosedive when you are manic.

Another thing about hypomania is that you are generally able to do more than you would normally do because you suddenly have boundless energy. It is nothing to be up at 3 in the morning rearranging all the books on the bookcase. Who needs to sleep? Certainly not you when there's so much to be done.

And projects seem so irresistible. Soon many different projects are in piles around the house, but most of them never get finished. I have many hobbies and interests and it is incredible the number of projects I can juggle at once. But as my hypomania progresses to mania, all sense of balance leaves me, and I find I cannot finish anything until the next episode of hypomania.

Your flight of ideas and speech are increased in hypomania, and eventually, people will not be able to follow what you are saying because you keep skipping off at tangents and interrupting everybody.

The mood in hypomania is generally euphoric and omnipotent, but some people, me included, are unlucky enough to have mixed episodes – features of depression and mania concurrently - where they are irritable and angry all the time. It is certainly a horrible state to be in. In my case, I have a lot of rage which is not pretty.

When a person transitions into full blown mania, they have similar symptoms as in hypomania but more acute, and downright alarming. Awareness goes out the window and so does reasoning. There is nothing logical about mania. It is not a time to be making decisions, or to try to concentrate on anything at all.

Speech and thoughts intensify. It is not easy for anybody to be around them at this stage. Sometimes the speech becomes completely unintelligible. The projects get out of hand, and the piles get higher and higher.

There is a complete lack of inhibition, especially sexually as people in mania are hyper-sexual and get into all kinds of sexual scrapes. They don't think twice about it at the time, and feel no guilt, but all that comes crashing down when their marriage falls apart and they find themselves in the divorce court.

Risk taking is a hallmark of mania and includes things like gambling, road rage, starting up questionable businesses, taking long trips abroad, huge shopping sprees, falling out with family and friends, and everything else that can wreck your life.

So, as you can see, mania is a merry dance that usually ends badly. The journey is fun, but the recriminations and apologies afterwards are not, and you suddenly look around and wonder where all your family and friends have gone. You are pretty much on your own after a manic episode.

I recently had my first manic episode and hurt a lot of people. Should I try to explain myself?

Welcome to bipolar mania! Oh, if I could go back and undo parts of my life that I have wrecked during my many manias I would, but life is not like that. Mania is unpredictable and uncontrollable. Things get said and done that we would never think of saying or doing under normal circumstances. Mania is dreadful.

With bipolar disorder comes an enormous amount of loss. We offend people, we upset family members, we lose control at work, we get rowdy at parties and we generally make a menace of ourselves. I am obnoxious, people tell me.

It is all par for the course. Bipolar is very difficult to live with.

I can't tell you how many times I have been in your position, and how many times I have gone back and apologized to people. Overall, I have found that people do not accept my apologies. I have called, written emails, even written long, handwritten letters all to no avail. People are fickle and they are also afraid of bipolar disorder. Stigma is still alive and well.

So, what can you do? The best thing you can do is work hard to get your bipolar disorder under control. That is easier said than done, I know, and it can take multiple med trials in order to get a little bit of peace from this illness.

Do keep on good terms with your psychiatrist, and get some therapy, if you are able. Also, take good care of yourself at home by getting enough sleep and a nutritious diet. Do some exercise and get out in the sunshine.

Hopefully, these measures will be enough to control your manic episodes, but if they do not you will need to prepare yourself for many broken relationships during your lifetime. If you get the medication right and you find a good therapist to talk to, you should find that you can control the mania to an extent, at least in the very beginning when you are still hypomanic. Even a loving friend or partner may be able to reign you in during your manias. But you will find that loving friends and partners are hard to come by if you have bipolar.

You might also like to try doing some mood charts to better predict your manias. You can get all kinds of charts on the Internet or on your phone. You can even make your own chart which is what I have had to do in the past due to mixed episodes and anxiety which are difficult to chart.

If you want to try to make amends, it may be worth it, but don't be surprised or disappointed if people do not come around to your way of thinking. It is the rare person who understands bipolar mania, and as I say, I have not found that people are forgiving.

Don't give up trying to get control of your mood swings. There is always hope when it comes to bipolar disorder.

Do you lack guilt while in a manic episode?

If you felt guilty, you wouldn't be manic. Simple as that. When in mania you don't think beyond your immediate desires. You don't think there is anything to feel guilty about. You are often impulsive and say hurtful things to people without thinking. You can spend your life savings at the casino and have indiscriminate sex with strangers, all this and more, but you still don't feel guilty.

People naturally hate being used or abused in any way, so even relatives and friends you have had for many years will not forgive your behavior when you are manic. People do not understand or accept the manic side of bipolar.

I have lost many friends and relatives due to mania. And so, I am sure, have you. If you have had any luck with apologies, then you are luckier than me. People do not accept apologies because they do not understand or want to understand bipolar mania. It is a very difficult problem with very few answers.

The only suggestion I have for avoiding mania is to always remember to take your medication on time and make sure you get enough sleep. Even a couple of nights without sleep can bring on a manic episode, so it is important to stick to a sleep schedule. Go to sleep and wake up at the same time every night, even on the weekends. Take a nap. Do what it takes to feel rested.

Also, it is very wise to cut down on drinking alcohol and taking drugs as both these things can interact with your medications making them ineffective.

You must remember that when you have bipolar you can no longer live a normal life. You need your sleep and need to always watch your behavior. It is just something you must learn to accept when you have this illness.

Bipolar, like diabetes, calls for a disciplined way of life. When you have diabetes, you must avoid eating sugary snacks or you will get sick. When you have bipolar you need to get enough sleep to avoid mania. Both bipolar and diabetes are lifelong illnesses with no cure. I usually object to the comparison between Bipolar and diabetes because people with diabetes do not change their personality when they are sick. I must admit, though, that they do indeed need to stick to a strict medication regimen and watch their lifestyle.

Hopefully, if you can keep mania at bay, you won't feel guilty about anything, and won't have to apologize to anyone.

Is it possible to appear totally normal during a manic episode?

I would say, no. There is so much going on inside a person's head when they are manic that it is not easy to hide it from other people.

For a start the person is all ramped up so they will be excitable, loud, inconsiderate, obnoxious, and oblivious to other people's feelings. It is easy to tell if somebody is having a manic episode when they are talking a mile a minute, interrupting everything you say, and generally making a fool of themselves.

It is also easy to note what they are doing - namely, taking risks. This can be alarming to the average person and they may want to jump in and stop the manic person from acting impulsively. However, this will not be met with gratitude because a person in mania does not like to be thwarted.

Risk-taking can involve many different things, but they are all impulsive and don't rely on reason or logic. For example, a person who is manic may spend many nights at the casino. They get so absorbed in the game they are playing that they don't think of the consequences and soon lose all their money.

Many people take risks by buying an excess of material goods. Somehow, they suddenly think they need things they don't have and buy up not one item but maybe ten or twelve. Ordering on the Internet has become a haven for people with bipolar mania and many things must be returned later. Much more serious financial risks are taken than just over-shopping, of course, and these can ruin people's lives.

Risk-taking also involves taking sudden long-distance trips, being missing for days, or indulging in promiscuous sexual activity with strangers.

Another thing that is very noticeable with manic episodes is people lose control of their speech and actions because their many thoughts are bombarding them all at once and are coming through the brain unfiltered. It is not uncommon to pick fights with people and say terrible things you would not normally say to them. Then, of course, you must try to repair the relationship afterwards when you are well, and many people are not at all forgiving when it comes to manic episodes.

What thoughts does a person have during mania?

It's not so much a thought, it is a knowing. Nobody needs to tell you that you are the most important person in the world, you just know it. Why you are not the President of the United States is a bit of a mystery, but you just assume that they made a mistake and didn't realize you were out there somewhere.

With severe mania that has gone into a psychotic phase, you literally think you ARE the President of the United States, or some other prominent character past or present. And how dare anybody try to persuade you otherwise.

It is a great feeling to be omnipotent. You can do anything you want, go where you want, say what you like. If you offend somebody, then it is their fault for being so thin-skinned.

If you were in any doubt before, you know now your life is the only one that matters. You wonder why you were foolish enough not to see it before. How could you have missed that fact?

You just know you deserve the best that life can offer. Why you have been denied it so far you can't imagine, and you want to correct that now before it is too late. Anybody that thwarts you should know better. How dare they even think you should be stopped when you are certain that you are the most important person in the world.

This means you can go out and buy all manner of things you have wanted for ages but thought you couldn't afford. You might buy up loads of new clothes, or maybe spend your money on expensive gadgets for the home.

You find casinos a great fascination, and it is nothing to throw down all your life savings at the roulette table. The fact that you can't afford the mortgage now doesn't even cross your mind.

The worst of it is living in this woe-begotten world where nobody appreciates you and everybody is stupid. They are so stupid you wonder why you have wasted time on them before. Now they are so maddening you want nothing to do with them.

People are infuriating. How dare they try to slow down your thoughts to their level. If you wanted to, you know you could beat them at any game. Your IQ is through the roof. You hardly even feature on the percentile. People like you are so rare that you should be recognized by society. You have no doubt you are the greatest human being who ever walked the earth. These are the thoughts of a person in mania.

Is bipolar mania an emergency?

Like depression, mania works in several stages.

I will give you some examples of how it affects me:

1. Initially, I am very happy and wouldn't consider it an emergency.

    For example, when I am initially in mania, I become hyper-sexual and think anybody that looks at me is doing so in a sexy way.

    I also feel excited so start talking and thinking very fast. My thoughts are clouded, and I begin to think I am super-human in some way. I have many ideas bombarding my brain at once, and begin all kinds of new projects.

    I visit stores and buy clothes and purses. I also start buying things for all my forthcoming projects. Paints and brushes for my art projects, and many DIY things because I am always improving my house when I am manic. I am Amazon's best customer.

Whether you consider the above an emergency is up to you, but not in my book. I certainly wouldn't welcome being carted off to the hospital because I bought ten purses.

2. Then everything begins to speed up, and I do things I wouldn't normally do.

    Last year I bought a room full of furniture. I needed it all, and didn't overspend, so was able to pay it back quite easily. Now, when I look back, I am pleased that I did that and do not feel it was a mistake.

    When the projects begin, I have bags of energy. I painted all my kitchen cabinets once and did many other big jobs in a couple of weeks. But when I ordered the stain for the cabinets, I ran out of energy and had to leave the staining for my next manic episode.

That is where my mania stops lately - I seem to have an inbuilt sense of balance.

3. In the past, I have had a rise in mania but don't consider this an emergency.

    I start driving very fast, and once overtook a semi without a thought for traffic coming towards me in the other lane. I could easily have crashed into the oncoming traffic or even knocked somebody off the pavement.

    I have also been in some very compromising sexual situations and risked unwanted pregnancy and STDs. Luckily, I was not married or in a steady relationship at the time, but I did not think about the consequences of my actions at all.

If things like these are considered emergencies, you must ask yourself how would you wrestle me to the ground and get me to the hospital. When mania takes hold, you feel so great it is impossible to admit you are ill.

4.   I have been in the last stages of mania and been hospitalized a number of times. I have no idea how I got there.

   I have no time to sleep, no time to eat, or do any of the things that normal people do. Time is at a premium. I become totally out of control and get very angry. I speak very fast, interrupt, speak loudly and may even become incoherent because my mind is so full of ideas. I get annoyed with people who can't keep up with me. Feeling highly elated is terrible in the end as it is impossible to keep up with your own mind.

I pace up and down the room, and my anger quickly turns to rage. That is when an emergency comes in because I am not longer able to function normally.

5.   I have had many episodes of psychosis which is the worst thing about bipolar 1.

   If my mania becomes totally out of control, I develop psychosis which is a medical emergency. At this stage, it is almost impossible to get me to the hospital without intervention as I have lost touch with reality. I will be hallucinating - seeing, hearing, and smelling things that are not there - and likely have paranoia. In my paranoid state, I will be thinking that people are out to harm me and are not trying to help me at all.

This is when the police have been called as I might do something to harm myself or somebody else.

Please note: These are my stages and are not official stages in mania. Some people do not recognize these stages at all.

Why are people with bipolar disorder hyper-sexual?

Hyper-sexuality is very common in bipolar disorder. It comes about in hypomania and mania, and is so common that it could be considered a normal symptom. Unlike depression where everything is slowed down, in mania everything is intensified.

When in hypomania or mania I feel sexy all the time and it is difficult to think about anything else. I think men are looking at me, which is a bit far-fetched at my age, and I think they are all dying to jump into bed with me.

In my youth I took it way too far and had some very dicey encounters. Fortunately, I was lucky and came away unscathed, but unwanted pregnancies or STDs can be the result of hypomania or mania.

This obviously has some very bad effects on current relationships, and when a partner has hyper-sexuality quite often this can inevitably lead to separation or divorce.

This symptom is often poorly understood by the medical profession and difficult to receive appropriate treatment for. Some doctors do not want to address this problem at all. None the less, treatment should be sought out because the obvious long-term dangers can be devastating.

I was once in a group therapy session in a hospital setting and the woman who ran it appeared to be a very strait-laced person who could easily be taken for an old maid. She wore very modest clothing, and no makeup, and her hair style was way out of fashion.

However, this strait-laced lady informed us all that she quite often got into trouble sexually. She would spend the night at parties, smoking pot and drinking, and would turn over in the morning and find she was in bed with somebody she didn't recognize. To say we were shocked was an understatement, but it just shows how this problem can affect anybody.

If you are prone to hyper-sexuality, and treatment has failed, it is advisable that you use contraception to avoid any surprise pregnancies. It can take a real toll on marriages and relationships, so it is better to get treatment as soon as possible.

Is it normal for someone having a manic episode to hurt someone's feelings?

Unfortunately, people having a manic episode hurt people's feelings all the time. Mania is very unpredictable, and you can never tell what you will say or do next. Thoughts are bombarding your mind all the time, day and night. It is like darts being thrown at your brain from all directions.

When manic, I get annoyed with people as I find that everybody appears to be walking and talking very slowly. They also seem to be saying and doing the most stupid things. It is common to judge everybody as stupid, but that is because the brain is working overtime. It is like a runaway train veering off the tracks. Speech and action come first - thoughts come much later when the manic episode is over.

When you come down to earth, and the train is parked in the station, you can be certain that you will be overcome with shame, guilt, and remorse for all the people you have upset and offended. Then comes all the letters and phone calls of apology, many of which will not be accepted because the average person cannot believe that a family member or friend could say or do such terrible things to them when they are supposed to love them. It is a difficult situation all round.

When mania subsides, it is very likely indeed that you will suddenly crash into a deep depression. The higher you go, the lower you fall. At this time, you will be wallowing in guilt, which is normal in depression, in any case. You just want to curl up and die when you think of all the terrible things you have said and done.

I live on my own, and rarely socialize, so I don't usually offend people when manic. However, my one brother has borne the brunt of many of my manias over the years because I always write what he calls my 'bipolar letters' and regret them later. He usually accepts that I can't help it, but once I offended him by something I said, and he wrote back saying he would have a very hard time forgiving me. Thank goodness he is very loving, kind person and is still speaking to me.

He suggested that I could write the letter then file it in the drafts folder of my email before sending it. This has proved to be a very useful solution to the problem, if and when I remember to do it!

Apart from this, I have said and done many other terrible things in the dim and distant past but do my best to forget them.

Can bipolar mania cause uncontrolled rage?

I have had many manic episodes and can tell you that I spent months in a permanent state of rage one year. Not irritability, not anger, but RAGE. It is embarrassing to admit to it.

There is something abhorrent about a woman in her 70s stomping back and forth, wringing her hands, shouting obscenities, and raging in her own home. Never mind the neighbors. Nobody here, nothing amiss, just rage tainting the air and sending my cat zooming under the bed petrified for his life.

It is totally amazing, even to me, that I could go from 0-10 in less than a second, be throwing things around the room (usually the phone), and banging my fist on the dining room table so hard that the evidence is apparent three months later.

RAGE is not nice.

It is not something that people willingly admit to. I was so ashamed of it that I even sat through an excruciatingly boring three weeks of an Anger Management course. I wrote in my notebook and did the exercises like all the other participants, yet at the end of the day, I was still filled with horrendous rage. There was no stopping me.

People say, nonchalantly, "Oh, you just have to take deep breaths and count to ten." These are the people who have absolutely no idea what rage is, or what it is like. It is beyond awful. It leaves you in floods of tears, shaking and sweating all over. If you have had rage, you will know what I am talking about.

In July I went to see my rather indifferent psychiatrist who scoffed at the idea of bipolar rage. You should be doing this and that, she said, followed by the suggestion that I should go away and not bother her. This treatment did me no good at all. I got even worse after that.

I used to dread getting up in the morning. Even before my feet touched the floor, I could feel the rage rising up from deep inside of me. Nothing had happened, I didn't have night-mares, my cat was sleeping peacefully at the foot of the bed. Yet there I was, this sweet little lady who looked as if she didn't have the strength to blow out a candle, vibrating from head to foot with rage.

I changed my psychiatrist - he at least acknowledged that there was such a thing as bipolar rage - he even sympathized with me. He wrote me up for an old anti-depressant (which is obviously not the answer for everyone). I drove to the pharmacy, with hope in my heart, my prescription clutched tightly in my hand.

Wow! That tiny, yellow pill made me human again. I have almost forgotten how rage nearly ruined my life. There is hope out there. Get the medication you need, and you will realize, once and for all, you are not that raving lunatic you once thought you were. You just had bipolar rage.

How do I stop spending urges with bipolar mania?

This is a serious problem with bipolar, and it is nothing to laugh about. Many people have let their spending habits get totally out of control and suffered greatly. Business ventures involving a lot of money have soured, spending on vacations have turned out badly, and some people have had to declare bankruptcy because they can't afford to pay their debts.

Spending too much money in mania can ruin marriages, and I would advise anybody who is about to be married to someone with bipolar 1 to consider this problem before it ruins their credit score and their relationship.

If one partner is a saver and the other one is a spender, things will go awry when the spending partner spends freely in mania. Then it is very difficult to patch up the relationship. If children are involved, this makes it even harder, and many marriages end up in the divorce courts with custody battles over the children.

One thing that might help you if you are the big spender is something I have done in the past when manic. It is very difficult to do, though. But if you can catch the mood before it gets out of control, you can put your credit cards in the safety deposit box at the bank.

My bank is very good when it comes to my illness. I have made friends with the bank manager and her assistant and they both help me control my money. They keep an eye on my bank balance every month, and if they see a lot of extra money going out, they bring it to my attention.

This is certainly not foolproof, but it does alert me to the fact that I have let my spending get out of hand. I usually get annoyed and defensive about the whole thing, but they are both very tolerant as they know it is my illness talking.

I have had some really bad manias and bought all kinds of things. One time I bought three cars in one week. Now it is a joke when I go to the bank. The bank manager says she looks out of the window when I arrive and sighs with relief when she sees my last car in the car park!

Car salesmen just love people with mania. They wait for us to pop in on one of our manic expeditions. I do my best to drive on by when I am in mania. But those shiny new cars all lined up in front of the dealership seem to lure me in.

Of course, these days many people shop online - Amazon is very happy to have me as a loyal customer. If I catch it in time, I put all the things in my cart into the 'Save for Later' file and never press the 'Proceed to Checkout' button until my mania is over. I generally end up with far too many items in my cart and must keep pressing the Delete button.

Otherwise, there's not much you can do because you are not thinking logically when you are happily squandering all your life savings. You can, perhaps, leave your credit cards with your partner, or somebody you can trust, but it is usually difficult to admit to overspending.

Can you feel sad during mania?

Bipolar with mixed features (or Dysphoric mania, as it used to be called) describes a manic state with symptoms of depression occurring at the same time. This means you could be loud and frenzied but feel sad and despondent at the same time. People with this condition feel on edge and dissatisfied with life even when their lives are going well.

It is a very serious condition as people are far more prone to risky behavior, and are in greater danger of suicide. To diagnose bipolar with mixed features, the doctor has to see 2 of 4 symptoms of depression and at least 1 symptom of mania.

DEPRESSIVE SYMTOMS:

- Sudden periods of crying for no apparent reason.
- Noticeable changes in sleep and appetite.
- Inability to make decisions.
- Anxious, irritable, angry, or worried.
- Body aches and pains.
- Wanting to self-harm, or thoughts of death and suicide.
- Wanting to isolate.

MANIC SYMPTOMS:

- Euphoria and self-importance.
- Needing less sleep or not feeling tired.
- Irritable and aggressive.
- Distracted.
- Engaging in risk-taking behavior.
- Delusions and hallucinations may occur.

Bipolar with mixed features is often difficult to treat. Mood stabilizers are used for mania or depression, so a medication, or combination of medications, must be found that will relieve symptoms of both. Much of the time anti-psychotics are used, but it often takes many trials to get the right dosage.

Every effort should be made to treat this side of bipolar disorder as the person feels anxious all the time and is inclined to take serious risks.

Do people with bipolar disorder miss mania?

Only people with Bipolar 1 have true mania. People with Bipolar 2 have hypomania which can be euphoric or charged with irritability. Many people have very productive hypomania's. They get a lot done and are often creative and fun to be around. If they are in management, their staff pay attention to them because they are full of ideas.

People with bipolar 2 have all the same symptoms as in a full-blown mania, but they are not taken to extremes. The person is aware of what is going on and they are often very entertaining and creative during their episodes.

I have bipolar 1 and know a lot of people with bipolar at my local mental health clinic. Although some people claim that they love mania, I have yet to meet anyone who enjoys mania to such an extent as to miss it.

I think the public has a mythical understanding of what mania is really like. They seem to think it is all about being ecstatic all the time and doing a lot of exciting things. Also, there are the adventures people hear about and secretly envy all those people in mania who are not afraid to take risks.

Mania may start off with a great exuberance for life but goes zooming off into Crazy Land before you can say 'mania'. You may enjoy a couple of great days of productivity, but that tragically comes to an end very quickly and the ravages of mania take hold.

Also, while you are having a manic episode you are not usually aware of it. It is only afterwards when you look back, usually in shock and horror, that you think about all the stupid things you have said and done when you were manic.

People in mania seem to get up to a lot of very questionable things. Many people spend so much money, especially buying things online, that they max out their credit cards in no time. Then, when they come down to earth, they realize that they have got to pay it all back.

Other people go even further than that and totally wreck their family's stability causing bankruptcies and evictions. Other people love to squander money at the casino or take impromptu trips around the world. They don't say anything to their partners half the time. One day, they just take off and are never seen again.

Then there is the road rage, the fights, the anger, and often the insults to everyone they love. Mania makes you boisterous and loud, you think everybody wants to listen to what you have to say, and there just isn't a filter on your tongue. Then, when you have totally alienated all your family and friends you have to go back and apologize later. I have found that people hardly ever accept my apologies after a manic episode and disappear out of my life for good.

And don't forget about the casual sex! When the metabolism is speeded up, everything becomes urgent, no holds barred, no guilt attached to it at all. So, many risky affairs are begun during mania leading to no end of trouble in marriages. Many end up in the divorce courts. And then there are the STDs and the unwanted pregnancies to worry about.

People with true mania usually wind up in the hospital if they do not come down from their manic state on their own. It is not unusual for people with Bipolar 1 to have several stays in the hospital. Bipolar 1 mania is disruptive, demoralizing, and often very expensive to rectify. Mania is like taking a wrecking ball to your whole life.

If someone has undiagnosed bipolar, and has their first manic episode, do they realize what they have done afterwards?

This is a complicated question because you are asking about an undiagnosed illness. We cannot guess what is wrong with a person., whatever symptoms they are experiencing, if they have not been given a correct diagnosis. It is not possible to say whether their symptoms are the result of bipolar disorder, or not.

Other things - like excessive drinking or taking street drugs - can lead to manic-like states, as can other physical and mental illnesses. Also, how would they know it is a manic episode if they have never had one before?

It is hard for a lay person to distinguish between hypo-mania and mania. They would really need to see a mental health professional to determine whether they have Bipolar 1 or Bipolar 2. People with Bipolar 1 have episodes of mania, whereas people with Bipolar 2 only have episodes of hypo-mania. Hypo-mania is a lesser form of mania but has the same symptoms and can be equally distressing.

Episodes of depression are not necessary for a diagnosis of Bipolar 1, but they are essential for a diagnosis of Bipolar 2. This is a very complicated illness, and is hard for a professional to diagnose, let alone somebody without mental health experience.

That being said, a person who has a manic episode will eventually stabilize, if not by themselves, then with medication. Mania is often self-limiting because it eventually uses up too much energy and the body succumbs to exhaustion from lack of sleep. The person often sinks into a deep depression immediately afterwards. However, some unlucky people have manias that go on for weeks, so it is not enough to generalize. Also, with Bipolar 1, psychosis is very possible in a manic or even a depressed state.

A severe mania can lead to a hospital stay if the person is out of control. This could be one of many hospital stays if the person is not receiving the correct treatment. This illness should be treated with mood stabilizers, and often other medications as well. It is very hard to treat it yourself at home. Without medication, the illness usually worsens.

As for the person realizing what they have done afterwards, that is a very big problem for most people who have a manic episode. Many things have been said and done in the heat of the moment, family and friends may well have disappeared, money might have been spent unwisely, and promiscuous behavior could lead to further trouble down the road. Mania is a cruel state to be in.

So, yes, they realize only too well, and often have a very hard time correcting and apologizing for all the mistakes they have made.

What advice would you give to a person who starts dozens of projects in mania and never finishes them?

I am exactly like you. I start many different projects when in bipolar mania. It is par for the course, and just another annoying symptom of bipolar disorder. I start thinking about writing projects I really should have done years ago, like collating all my poetry and putting it on the computer. I also go back to old novels I was writing or start new ones. At first, it is great fun, but when the mania subsides all the fun goes out of it and it soon becomes drudgery.

I am also an artist, so tend to start many different paintings when in mania. I have many half-finished oils and watercolors stacked up against the wall. However, I am lucky enough to have a studio in my house where I can leave out my art supplies and do a little bit every now and then when the mood strikes.

I have found an answer to the art projects now, and am drawing in colored pencils. I bought hundreds of colored pencils on the Internet in one of my manias, but now find it very satisfying to copy pictures on Pinterest while I am watching TV. Since colored pencils take up very little room, it is not a problem anymore. I can draw on my lap in my recliner.

If I were you, I would just have fun and not let it bother you. Pile up your projects for later. There are far more serious side effects to worry about when you are manic. Many creative people love mania because they can be so productive.

What's the difference between mania and anxiety?

At the outset, some people do claim they have a lot of anxiety with mania, but I have never been able to understand this. My friend, who also has bipolar 1, tells me that when she feels her anxiety rising, she knows she is becoming manic. Since I have never felt this way, or indeed known that I am becoming manic, I simply cannot understand it.

To me mania, even hypo-mania, is either a euphoric or dysphoric state, i.e., there is a great deal of energy behind the state of mania.

When you are in a euphoric state you think you are Super Man or Super Woman and can do anything better than anybody else. You can even paint a picture and have it hung in the Louvre if you put your mind to it. People who don't believe that are just plain ignorant. That is how people in euphoric mania think.

Dysphoric mania is very different, but nowhere near as common. When in dysphoric mania you have a great deal of energy just like euphoric mania but it is directed towards irritability and anger. It is a dreadful state to be in because your every waking hour is spent in anger. Even when you wake up in the morning, when nothing in particular has happened to annoy you, your anger is still with you. If your anger gets out of control you will undoubtedly go into a rage which is unstoppable.

So, when I think of bipolar mania and anxiety, I just cannot put the two together. In euphoric mania there is a strong sense of omnipotence, and in dysphoric mania there is a feeling of extreme anger. Both, to me, take up a lot of energy. You are like the Energizer Bunny emitting strong vibes wherever you go. People run and seek cover when you enter a room because they are afraid of mania and have no idea how to cope with a person in that state.

Anxiety, on the other hand, is a loss of energy. A feeling of being too scared to breathe, a feeling of extreme fright that something terrible is about to happen. You shake all over, your heart bangs, you sweat and you just want to run away. It is a horrible feeling. With these thoughts in mind, I can't understand how the two can possibly co-exist. If you do understand this, you are experiencing something different from me.

PART SIX
Psychosis

What is psychosis and how does it happen?

Psychosis is not an illness in itself, but a state of being caused by another illness, physical or mental. It is what happens when a person loses touch with reality. They will wonder whether what they are thinking and feeling is real or not.

The problem is they can get no confirmation from those around them as other people say they are not thinking or feeling the same things. It is very frightening to be on the outside of humanity looking in. It is like other people have a secret they are not telling you about. It can make you feel very lonely. When you are psychotic, you are living in your own little world and it seems 100% true to you.

Psychosis affects the senses; therefore, it interferes with what you see, hear, smell, touch, and taste. It also affects your thinking. You become very confused which is natural if you are experiencing things that others are not. It also affects your concentration and cognition. It is difficult to understand concepts, and things just do not make sense to you when you are psychotic. This can make a person very anxious and agitated as their whole world is upside down.

People who are psychotic don't sleep well or enjoy their food, and they have limited interest in personal hygiene. They generally cut themselves off from society and isolate no matter how other people may try to include them in what is going on in the real world. They may self-harm or harm others because one of their voices tells them to hurt people. The hallmarks of psychosis are hallucinations and delusions.

Hallucinations involve the senses. A person who is psychotic will be able to hear things like people's voices - shouting, screaming, whispering - and think they are real. They will usually experience seeing strange things that do not make sense at all. They might smell smoke, feel things crawling all over their skin, or think various foods taste like metal or plastic.

Delusions involve thinking, or cognition. Psychosis can make you believe your neighbors have bugged your house or the CIA is plotting to kill you, or special messages are coming out of the television just for you. The problem is nobody else believes this to be true. This makes the person more on edge than before and, nobody can dissuade them, as their beliefs are unshakable.

Psychosis happens to many people. In fact, one in five people will have some form of psychosis in their lifetime. This is a very large number. It can be brought on by physical illnesses like Huntington's and Parkinson's, medication, drug or alcohol abuse, brain tumors, stroke and mental illnesses like schizophrenia or bipolar disorder.

People with bipolar 1 are more susceptible to psychosis than others, while people with Bipolar 2 have reported psychosis on occasion. More than 50% of people with bipolar 1 will have an episode of psychosis in their lifetime.

Some people, particularly those with Bipolar, have brief episodes of psychosis which have a very short prodromal phase, but other people, like those with Schizophrenia, suffer psychosis much of the time, although this can be lessened with anti-psychotics.

Can bipolar be defined as a psychotic disorder?

Bipolar disorder is a very complex mental illness. It is classified as a mood disorder, not a psychotic disorder, and is referred to as such by the medical community. Unlike unipolar depression (major depressive disorder), which has only depressive moods, bipolar has moods of depression and hypomania or mania.

No definitive cause has yet been found for bipolar disorder, and there is no cure either. However, it can be managed in most cases with medication, therapy, and lifestyle changes. There are no blood tests or x-rays that can prove bipolar exists in the brain, there is only the patient's history on which to make a diagnosis.

A person can be diagnosed with bipolar 1 or bipolar 2. People with bipolar 2 have hypo-mania which is a less extreme form of mania but with the same symptoms. There are other forms of bipolar disorder on the bipolar spectrum, but they do not include psychosis.

People with bipolar 1 can have psychosis with acute mania or depression. Psychosis is terrible at the best of times, but at least people with bipolar go back to a manic, depressive, or euthymic mood after a psychotic episode. A few people with bipolar 2 have reported episodes of psychosis but that is rare and may require a new diagnosis of bipolar 1.

Schizophrenia, unlike bipolar, is classed as a psychotic disorder as the person experiences many psychotic episodes in their lifetime. This illness can be alleviated somewhat by medication, but many people still hallucinate and have delusions despite the best medication cocktail. It is quite common for the person to still hear voices even when anti-psychotics are given.

Are psychotics born or made?

People with psychosis are not born with it, and neither is it 'made' during their lifetime. Those with schizophrenia or schizoaffective disorder are most often prone to psychosis, in fact that is an essential part of the diagnosis. They often hear voices from people who are not there, they hallucinate, and they think people are out to cause them harm. These symptoms (psychosis) can abate to some extent with medication. Or the person learns to live with them.

Psychosis is also a common symptom of bipolar 1. Over half the people with bipolar 1 will experience psychosis at some time in their lives. The symptoms are the same as in schizophrenia, but are generally temporary. They usually occur in severe manic or depressive episodes and last for days or weeks, although some people get symptoms of psychosis that last for much longer periods.

In neither of these cases, schizophrenia or bipolar, is psychosis present at birth because these disorders do not usually appear until the early teens or twenties. (Some children are found to have these illnesses, but they are not born with psychosis either).

Psychosis is sometimes found in major depressive disorder and organic brain disorders like Parkinson's, brain tumors, and Huntington's Disease. It can also occur temporarily with alcohol and drug abuse because these two behaviors affect the brain. Some elderly people suffer with temporary psychosis as well if they are given very strong medications in the hospital.

It is also thought that, in some circumstances, a period of extreme stress can cause psychosis, but this is rare.

Can psychosis be temporary?

I have had many periods of psychosis (I have lost count) due to bipolar 1 disorder, and I can tell you they have all been temporary. Some people experience psychosis for extended periods, but even so, in bipolar 1 they are temporary otherwise I would still be psychotic.

Many say they have experienced psychosis with bipolar 2. I don't doubt them, but I do doubt their diagnosis. It is said that only people with bipolar 1 experience psychosis, so logically speaking their diagnosis should be changed to bipolar 1. And it often is changed to this.

People with schizophrenia have great difficulty in terms of psychosis because schizophrenia is a psychotic illness. They often have very long bouts of psychosis which can be very destructive to their life. There are very good anti-psychotics on the market to help people with resistant psychotic symptoms, and many people with schizophrenia have gone into remission. However, the problem is some people stop taking their medications then they can get even worse.

It is very common for people with mental illnesses to stop taking their medication, and this is even more common in people with schizophrenia. They may be given their medication by others, but quite often they hide them and do not take them.

My psychoses have lasted for several days or weeks, in most cases, and ended when I was admitted to the hospital. I remember one psychotic episode was resistant to treatment and lasted for about six weeks. Sometimes, my psychoses went away without any treatment at all.

Psychosis is a very disturbing state to be in, but is fortunately something that can usually be corrected with the right medications. Some people with schizophrenia get breakthrough symptoms despite medications, and they have no choice but to learn to live with it. Often, this takes the form of voices, usually derogatory voices, mocking them or demanding that they commit violent acts.

I never had voices telling me what to do but did experience a lot of hallucinations like seeing and smelling things that weren't there. I also heard choirs singing in my head, and sometimes my name being called which was rather disturbing. I used to dash outside to see who had come to the door, but no one was there.

Bipolar psychosis can come on with severe manic or depressive episodes, but it is usually only temporary. It is generally termed mood-congruent or mood incongruent according to whether it manifests in conjunction with the current mood the person is experiencing.

How do you cope with the realization that you have psychosis?

When you become psychotic, you often realize there is something wrong. You may see things or hear things other people don't see or hear. Perhaps you think people on the street are making some gesture that has meaning for you. You may smell something other people don't smell. Or you may hear strange voices in your head.

This can be very disturbing and confusing, and you start to question it. If you leave it, and don't confide in someone, you are missing a chance to recover early and may well become deeply psychotic as time goes by. Then it is more difficult to treat.

Quite often your situation is first noticed by others. For example, your parents may notice when you are at home, or your peers when you are an adult. If they express concern, it is wise to try to explain what is happening to you so that you can get some help.

The first signs of psychosis may benefit from therapy like cognitive behavioral therapy (CBT), or talk therapy, but as time goes by and the symptoms worsen, medication is usually needed. Anti-psychotics are very helpful for psychosis and it is best to get started on them as early as possible because they can take some time to work.

If you allow the psychosis to develop further, you will not be aware of what is happening to you at all so will not be able to cope with the situation. When things worsen, and you are having regular hallucinations and delusions, you will not be able to recognize if something is real or not. So, if you are aware that something is not quite right, seek treatment right away.

What are the prodromal signs of psychosis?

The prodromal signs of an illness are the things that occur before the illness takes hold. When talking about psychosis, these signs are very vague and often go unnoticed, especially by the person, although friends and relatives may think that something is wrong.

Prodromal signs are usually more noticeable in schizophrenia because their psychoses are generally much longer than in those of bipolar 1. These signs can appear long before the psychosis occurs, often months or years before.

The signs and symptoms are as follows:

- Consistently worrying about grades at school, or job performance.

- Struggling to think straight or concentrate.

- Having unwarranted suspicion of others.

- Failure to keep up with personal hygiene.

- Withdrawing from friends and family.

- Experiencing strong, inappropriate feelings, or no feelings at all.

These symptoms are not unlike hormonal symptoms in adolescence, and that is the time when these illnesses manifest in young people. This can be very confusing, even to the mental health professionals.

If there are prodromal sigs of psychosis in bipolar 1, they often go unnoticed as the psychosis often comes on rapidly. People with bipolar 1 usually have brief episodes, although some people have experienced psychoses that have gone on for weeks or months.

Can someone with psychosis lead a normal life?

I have had many psychotic episodes in my lifetime (none for the past few years, thank goodness). Was it possible for me to lead a normal life when psychotic? That is debatable.

I seem to remember doing normal things, like getting up, brushing my teeth, eating my breakfast etc. but these were just rote activities that take little thought. If I tried to read a book, for example, it was impossible for me to concentrate because my brain was filled with extraordinary thoughts and hallucinations.

Let me see if I can remember one or two things that happened: I was watching TV one night, just a casual night, when I saw an commercial for Theraflu come on. I have seen that commercial many times before, but this time the man who came into the room had horns coming out of his head. I remember studying him and thinking that it was strange, but it didn't worry me much.

A similar thing happened when I went to see a new psychiatrist. I walked into his office, sat down and there he was on the other side of the desk with horns coming out of his head. Now this affected me more than the man on TV. Why? I don't know. Maybe, it was because he was a real person, or maybe I recognized that he was somebody who was trying to help me and I didn't think he would be able to do much if he was the Devil.

However, the fact that I was able to drive to his office showed that I was functioning normally, but you couldn't say that I was leading a normal life.

Once I went out for dinner with a friend. We were eating our meal, I looked down, and there were hundreds of cockroaches walking around on the floor. I found this quite interesting and studied them closely. I mentioned it to my friend, but she just laughed. Now was I leading a normal life? It depends on how you look at it. I was out with a friend having dinner, so that was normal, but if I was seeing these cockroaches then I was obviously ill.

Another time when I saw bugs – I'll keep the observations similar - was in a half-way house, having come out of the hospital the day before. I shouldn't have been in the half-way house at all because I was sicker there than when I went into the hospital a month before. When I went to bed there was no problem at all, but in the middle of the night I woke up and saw that the floor was covered in little black beetles - thousands of them all milling about. This time I was alarmed, so I shot out of bed, petrified, and went to see the warden (who was fast asleep). She hurried to my room and became angry with me for waking her up because she couldn't see any beetles anywhere.

Now, I was able to walk about, eat my food, have a conversation (albeit rather a bizarre one) with this woman, but I was obviously not leading a normal life.

I don't think I have a definitive answer to this question except to say that psychosis varies from time to time and from person to person. It is easy to live life normally, but your head is full of chaos that is not apparent to other people.

How do you explain to people you have just met that you have a psychotic disorder?

If I were you, I would steer clear of any explanations, especially if you have just met someone. Imagine if you were presented with such information. It is almost guaranteed that your relationship will not even get off the ground.

Let's say you had just met somebody, and they told you they had an STD. Would you want to get to know that person? I don't know if that would bother you, but I would find it a conversation stopped. It is the same with psychosis. People do not understand it, and nor do they want to in most cases. Please try to restrain this urge because, more than likely, it will not work out well for you.

Even if you have known someone for a long time you would not say anything to them either, unless they were able to help you deal with it. It is debatable whether to tell family members, or not, as many people can turn on you because they are not familiar with something as serious as psychosis. It is unfortunate, but many people shun relatives or friends who have mental illnesses, and there is often nothing to do but accept it.

People are not all psychiatrists, and have no business knowing such intimate details about your life. You must remember that there is still a great deal of stigma attached to psychosis, mainly because people do not understand it and are afraid.

Also, the average person does not want to understand psychosis. Some people even think it is contagious so would probably run a mile given this information. Other people are convinced it is caused by demons, or is the work of the Devil. Of all the mental illnesses, psychosis probably has the worst reputation of all due to films like 'Psycho' and mass shootings.

These things influence the public and cause a great deal of fear, whereas most people with psychosis are usually gentle and harmless. I know your need to 'confess' is paramount in your mind, but it will do more harm than good. People talk, and you will find they are ignoring you.

On the other hand, if you have a psychotic episode and you have somebody you can trust in your life, then it would be wise to share this information with them because they may be able to help you. You must choose your allies carefully as this disclosure can severely affect your life.

At what point does a belief become a delusion?

Beliefs differ from person to person. We are not born with beliefs - they are handed down by those closest to us. If your parents are very religious then, chances are, you will grow up to be a believer yourself. As an adult, you will more than likely attend the same church or Synagogue.

Political beliefs are another thing. Many people are brought up to believe in one political party or the other. It is common for adults to be very intolerant of people of a different political persuasion which creates a lot of ill will and division in society.

Some people believe that "money doesn't grow on trees" which makes it very difficult should they marry a person who thinks you should "live and let live." While one is out spending money and running up their credit cards, their partner is at home playing *Scrooge*. Beliefs like these can easily clash and the marriage may end in divorce.

Some of these beliefs are good and bring great comfort to people in their everyday lives. Some are bad and confusing. But who is to say what is good and what is bad anyway? Beliefs are very personal.

Whether you ever question your beliefs is another issue entirely. Many/most people never think to investigate the beliefs they have inherited, and some really suffer for the rest of their lives. Many families scare their children into believing what they believe to be true, and the child grows up in fear. Children are very susceptible to the words of their parents and other authority figures, so it is important that people question their own beliefs before passing them on.

Many people have unusual beliefs that seem totally ridiculous to the rest of the world; think about all the religious cults for a start. It is hard to believe in a person like David Koresh or Jim Jones, but many people did just that and lost their lives in the process. That is the thing about beliefs; they are very real to the person who is experiencing them.

There are also people who believe that the President is the Devil, and the Speaker of the House is a Witch. They can create all kinds of trouble with their beliefs and may even sink to violent or immoral behavior.

When a belief crosses the line and becomes a delusion is debatable. A delusion is generally considered a symptom of a mental illness. It is something a person must live with if their illness includes episodes of psychosis. Psychosis means a complete break from reality. The person is not living in the world as you or I know it - they are living in their own little world which they believe to be true although it is not. People with delusions are almost always terrified of something or someone. And those terrors are often bizarre and unbelievable to others.

It is quite common for people to have delusions that their neighbors are bugging their walls, or the CIA has sent people to spy on them, or radio stations are telling them to kill their family members. That's when delusions turn deadly.

I know a college student, who believed his mother had poisoned his fish. He was so deluded about this that he stabbed her to death. He stabbed himself, too, and had to spend the rest of his life in a mental hospital. It was only there he received the diagnosis of schizophrenia. This was overlooked before this incident because the boy was so intelligent. He was completing his Master's in biology at a university at the time. Nobody considered anything was wrong with him. Yet his own mind was deceiving him.

Some people, especially those with bipolar 1, have delusions of grandeur where they believe they are a famous person, either in present day or back in history. Not everybody who is psychotic has delusions, but when they do it can become all consuming.

Where these beliefs become delusions is debateable.

Can a person suffer after a delusion?

I am not sure what you mean by suffer after a delusion. If you mean, does a person suffer mentally or physically that would depend on the person. In most cases the suffering is the delusion and takes place while the delusion is in progress. If you mean, is a person able to repair the damage they have caused through their delusion, then I would have to say not in all cases.

Although I have experienced many hallucinations, with bipolar disorder, as far as I can remember, I have only experienced two delusions. The worst one, and the one that did the most harm to myself and another person, was when I began to get very suspicious of my best friend. She and I did everything together, and we had a marvelous relationship, but I lost touch with all that when I began doubting her and her actions.

At first, I thought she had stolen things from me, then I began to think she had left the gas unlit on my stove to poison me. (My house is all electric!) Then I thought she was doing something strange in my garden even though she was being helpful by cutting my grass.

When I went into the hospital to have a colonoscopy, she sat with me because it took me three hours to come round. When I came home, I began to think that the reason I hadn't come round was because she had injected something into my IV bag, and I could have died.

I never said anything to her but began to keep my distance. Then one night I heard my door handle turn in the bedroom when I was in bed. I got up, but there was nobody there. Then I looked in the garden and thought I saw her doing things behind a bush.

I flew out of my house, (thank goodness I thought to get dressed), drove to the police station and wrote out a lengthy report of all the crimes I thought she had committed against me. I told the police about the bedroom door being rattled and the shadows behind the bush, so to prove me wrong they drove me to her house at three in the morning. When we arrived, they felt the hood of her car which was stone cold. That was supposed to have dissolved my delusion, but it did not, and I ended up spending a month in a mental hospital trying to come back down to earth.

When my friend found out that I had gone to her house with the police, she stopped speaking to me. By this time, I was out of the hospital so wrote her a very long letter of apology which was ignored. I felt sad about that because she has a brother with schizophrenia, and I thought she would understand. That was the end of a good friendship.

So, as you can see, a delusion is so real to the person that their beliefs cannot be shaken. And, yes, it does cause suffering after the event.

How can you tell if you are manic or psychotic?

I have bipolar 1 and have had many manic episodes during my lifetime. I can honestly say I didn't realize I was manic while it was happening but could remember it quite clearly afterwards. Usually, other people are aware of it because it is difficult to hide.

If you have a manic episode, here are some symptoms you may recall later:

•	A need to talk very fast and not be interrupted.

•	Many ideas coming into your mind at once.

•	Taking on different projects but not finishing them.

•	No interest in sleeping for days with no ill effects.

•	Not having time to sit down and eat a proper meal.

•	Taking big risks, you wouldn't normally take, like those with finances, relationships, or sexual affairs.

I was unable to recognize anything when I was in a psychotic episode because I had lost touch with reality. Everything I experienced took place in a fantasy world.

I hallucinated which meant that only I could see, hear, and smell things that other people couldn't experience.

I had delusions as well, believing that a story was true when it was not. This sometimes included paranoia where I believed someone or something was watching me and threatening me with my life.

I was able to realize that I was experiencing psychosis after the event but could not recognize it while it was taking place. However, I have heard of people who have realized they were psychotic while it was happening, and they were able to question their experiences and give them a reality check. This seems to apply to people with schizophrenia who have been ill for many years. They are so used to their psychotic experiences that they can question them while they are happening.

As to whether you can tell the difference between these states in bipolar 1, I would have to say you would not be able to tell because you would be oblivious in both cases.

What strange things happened to you during psychosis?

I can't say I think about anything in particular when I step into Wonderland. I accept that things are sometimes strange, but I don't question them. The landscape is different - everything is very bright and sometimes the colors hurt my eyes. The people, if there are any, are very annoying. They often walk slowly and get in my way.

On one occasion, when I was driving down the road, I saw a notice on a billboard outside a church that I thought was intended for me personally. It said, "You are very wicked, Sally." I didn't think anything of it at the time, and just accepted it at face value.

One alarming thing I remember, though, was hearing a voice coming out of my computer. It was talking directly to me and no matter what I did, I couldn't shut it up. I turned off the computer and closed the lid, but the voice kept talking to me, so I left the room to get away from it. I was very frightened that time.

I often find when I am psychotic everything is repeated. I always have the TV on because I am on my own. I often hear the exact same word or phrase on TV at the same time as I am reading it in a book or typing it on my computer. It is not just ordinary words or phrases,either, but strange things you wouldn't normally say. I still think it is real, but my psychiatrist thinks it has to do with my psychosis.

I don't hear people talking to me, but when it is very quiet, I can hear a group of people laughing or singing. I am sure they are laughing at me and it upsets me.

I also smell things like smoke when I am psychotic. I go around the house sniffing the air but cannot find anything burning. The fact that I have electricity and smoke detectors doesn't register with me, I still smell smoke in all the rooms. I have called the Fire Department a few times and they come out and check everything as part of their job. But although they don't find anything burning, it does not alleviate my anxiety. Then when I go to bed, I can smell the smoldering sheets and can't get to sleep.

I see things that other people don't see. They do not seem strange when in a deep psychosis, and they are not usually frightening. Most of the time I just accept that they are there.

I was once being driven by my friend through a forested housing estate at night and saw silver deer leaping out of the trees. I brought this to her attention, and she kept looking, but had no idea what I was talking about.

When I was taken to the hospital one year, and had to wait in the waiting room, I started pacing up and down and saw my shadow 50 feet long pacing in front of me. It was weird and very scary.

The strangest most unnerving thing to me is seeing bugs. When I visited my very first mental hospital many years ago, I saw them everywhere. I could be sitting down eating my meal, and there would be huge bugs all around my feet. I was sure I would step on them if I moved my feet, but I just accepted that there would be bugs on the floor in a hospital.

When you talk about strange thoughts during delusions, that is a different matter. I have only had two episodes as far as I can remember, but the most bizarre one was when I thought my psychiatrist was being very suggestive towards me.

One time in his office, I told him I had my own business called Sort it Out and had clients all over town. I told him I went to their houses and sorted out their garages, closets, toy rooms, offices etc. He reacted in a strange way, and in my mind, I thought he referred to my clients as if I was a prostitute. I remember him asking about my behavior on the streets. He wanted to know how I picked up men, how many did I take to my home, did I perform strange acts with them, and did I use a dildo.

I was appalled by this line of questioning and denied everything, trying to explain to him that my clients were people I worked for in their homes. I kept mulling this over that night, then the next day I went to his office and put a press cutting on his desk - I had been interviewed by the local newspaper that week and there was a photo of me on the front page and an article that talked about my clients who were everyday housewives.

That doctor left the clinic before I could see him again, and the doctor who took his place sat with his door open at my next visit.

Now, I have to ask myself if that was a delusion, or was the doctor really suggestive. What conclusion would you come to? I have no idea to this day.

Can depression cause psychosis?

Psychosis affects bipolar 1 and very occasionally major depressive disorder and other illnesses. It used to be thought that people with bipolar disorder only have psychosis stemming from a manic episode. This is the usual case, but they can also have psychosis stemming from a depressive episode. It is the severity of the illness that causes psychosis.

However, there is another difference in psychosis. It can be either mood-congruent or mood-incongruent. This means that the psychosis may, or may not, corresponds to the mood.

For example, if a person is manic, you would expect their psychosis to display manic tendencies, as in feeling that they have been sent from heaven to put the world right, or indeed they might think that they are Jesus himself who has risen again. If they are mood-incongruent, however, they could easily feel distraught because they believe they have murdered a whole nation of people.

If a person is in depression when they become psychotic, you would expect them to feel guilty, for example, for upsetting their family. You would not expect them to be laughing when their dog has died.

This difference is very important when it comes to psychiatric care. The treatment for psychosis is generally anti-psychotics, and often a hospital stay. Most psychoses will resolve in a matter of days or weeks, but some episodes are more drug-resistant and can take many months to recover from.

What is the difference between psychosis and psychopathy?

These two conditions often get confused as they sound alike. They are both given bad press, but they have little in common. Psychosis is a state of being caused by a severe physical or mental illness, while psychopathy describes a personality disorder. Psychosis is always found in schizophrenia as this is a psychotic disorder. But it can also be the result of a manic or depressive episode in bipolar 1.

When a person is psychotic it means they have lost touch with reality. They have hallucinations and delusions that other people can't verify. This condition is treated with anti-psychotics and/or a hospital stay. It is not a permanent condition in bipolar disorder as it only appears when a manic or depressive episode is severe. Although it is usually treatable medically, it is sometimes self-limiting.

Psychopathy and sociopathy, on the other hand, refer to Anti-social Personality Disorder (ASPD). Although these are classed as mental illnesses, the person is not sick in the usual way. It is just their normal personality.

People who are psychopathic are thought to be born with that condition. That means their whole life is spent with certain personality traits. They are often charismatic and charming and can convince people of the most unbelievable things. They are convincing liars, as well, and are the con men of society.

Their distinct lack of empathy often leads them to commit heinous crimes without any sense of remorse, and the condition is not corrected by punishment. These are the people who harm animals and other children when they are young, then sometimes grow up to harm others.

People with sociopathy have very similar traits, but the difference is they do, on occasion, suffer from remorse. This condition is thought to be nurture rather than nature so is learned behavior in childhood. Neither condition is treatable with medications although psychotherapy has been known to help. The problem is, if a person has either one of these conditions, they don't think they are ill so are unlikely to go for treatment of any kind.

PART SEVEN
Anxiety & panic attacks

Although anxiety is not a symptom of Bipolar Disorder, over 50% of people with this condition also have anxiety.

Do anxious people live in the future?

I have bipolar disorder so know about depression and mania. I also have social anxiety disorder and panic attacks. Many people with bipolar have anxiety. It is very common.

Thinking about your question, I can see that people who have anxiety do indeed live in the future. Some live with anxiety and worry about how their life will turn out, or they worry about a particular thing. Whatever the question, anxiety is all about fear.

They fear so many things that it makes life unbearable. They often fear being in social situations, speaking out loud, or writing something in front of other people. I know all about that myself and have concocted all kinds of tricks in the past to avoid people watching me fill in forms or even speak on the telephone.

Now I always fill in forms in pencil first, then go back and write over the answers in ink. That saves a great deal of anxiety. Also, when I meet someone, I introduce myself and say their name out loud so that I won't forget it.

When I think about depression, I can see that people who are depressed usually live in the past. They ruminate about all the things that have happened to them and all the bad choices they have made. They also worry about how they appeared to others, what they said, and how they mishandled things in the past. Again, I have had my fair share of that, and have worried about the stupid things I said and did in the past.

It is obviously a fruitless worry as the past is done and you cannot change it. The future is not here yet, so you cannot do anything about that either.

If we were disciplined, we would be able to live in the present all the time as that is the only place that is safe from anxiety and depression. We cannot live any other way. But most people never succeed in living in the present as it is very difficult to do and takes all our concentration.

But what of people like you, and half the people with bipolar who have depression and anxiety to put up with? That's the question you should be asking yourself now. Do you live in the past or do you live in the future? You obviously can't live in both at the same time, but the disorders do co-exist.

If you would like to read more about living in the present, you can read the Best Seller by Eckert Tolle called *"The Power of Now."*

How do I stop worrying?

I am a worrier too. I think if most people were honest, they would admit to worrying, as well. It is natural to worry about things because there is just so much to worry about these days.

People worry about their relationships, their finances, their health, race relations, the environment, the Government, the weather and just about everything else. We live in very uncertain times and some people worry more than others.

When I start to worry, I generally write down all my problems in one column and write beside them what I am going to do about it. Then I do what I can. Quite often problems resolve themselves. Or they just never happen.

You could try journaling. Just write whatever comes into your head. Make lists of all your worries, don't stop to correct the grammar or the spelling, just write until you can't think of anything else to worry about.

Another thing you might like to try is taking some time out to worry. Every day take half an hour or so and sit down and worry. Yes, worry all you can for that allotted time. When the half hour is up, go about your business as usual.

Some problems seem far too great or urgent, though, and must be solved right then and there. No point worrying about those things, you just have to take care of them.

Here are the things I am worrying about today:

I have just had my kitchen and two bathrooms painted and there is a dreadful mess in the house. I can hardly move. I am worried about this because I am getting old and have a lot of health problems, so, I need to find somebody to help me clean it up. I tried three different people, but nobody is available. I can see I shall end up doing it myself tomorrow.

At the same time as this inside work is being done, I have two other men working on hail storm damage on the outside of my house. I am worried about what they are doing out there and if they are doing everything properly. I have to keep popping outside to make sure that they are doing everything I want.

I have two new cats who are both wonderful, but they absolutely hate each other so I worry about them all the time. It is hissing and yowling all day and I don't think they will ever get on together. I worry they will start fighting and I will have to take them to the vet because they are injured. And I am worried that I may have to give up one of them.

I appreciate where you are coming from. If I were to say, 'Don't worry' it wouldn't make any difference, would it? When you are a worrier, you are a worrier. No two ways about it.

But I shall sit down tonight and make my worry list. I hope you will do the same.

Should I be taking something for pain to treat the symptoms of a panic attack?

I am sorry to hear that you are having panic attacks. I know from experience how debilitating they are.

As you know, panic attacks not only mess with your mind leading you to think you are surely going mad or are about to die on the spot, but they also have many unpleasant physical symptoms too.

Along with the fear of madness and death you can't catch your breath, and your heart is banging so hard it feels like it is about to jump out of your chest. Also, as you probably know, you break out in a cold sweat and your hands start to shake. It is also normal to have chest pain when you are having a panic attack and there are many other physical symptoms as well.

You also know that when you are having a panic attack it can feel as if you are having a heart attack. The symptoms are the same. Indeed, the medical profession can never be sure if you are having a heart attack or not without doing tests. The pain in the chest can be unbearable at times.

All this has led me to the emergency room more than once. Whilst there, you are treated with speed and efficiency - your blood is drawn, you have an EKG and even a chest Xray. All these tests are done within a matter of minutes because speed is of the essence if you are indeed having a heart attack.

Of course, when they declare that there is nothing wrong with you physically it is embarrassing, and you ask yourself why you got into such a panic in the first place. However, I have been told more than once, that they are only doing their job. If you are having a heart attack it is no use sitting at home waiting to die.

My advice to you is not to wait around to see if a pain killer will work (that could take 20 mins. to half an hour, and won't do anything for a heart attack), but if your symptoms are really bad call 911 and ask for advice. They will almost certainly call the ambulance, and before you know it you are in the E.R. with all manner of things going on around you.

If they find it was a panic attack (I won't say JUST a panic attack) you will be able to relax, and if they do find that you have had a heart attack at least you will be in the right place.

How would you deal with thoughts that cause anxiety?

The reason why most people get anxious is because they don't realize the natural cycle of:

- **THOUGHT**
- **FEELING**
- **ACTION**

A thought always pops into your mind before a feeling. Once you think the thought you feel the feeling and act on it or otherwise.

If your thoughts are negative, which I would hazard a guess and say they are, then you have a negative feeling. You may act upon that in many different ways.

The answer to this is to catch yourself in the thought process and stop it so that the feeling is positive, not negative. I say this, as if it is easy, but it is not. Especially if you are the kind of person who has been thinking negatively for a long time. So, never be hard on yourself if you find it hard to stop your thoughts and change the way you think.

Negative self-talk is really common, that's why there are so many people suffering from anxiety, and anxiety related problems. Some people have generalized anxiety where their self-talk is so negative that they cause a tremendous amount of worry all day and every day. It is self-defeating.

You might like to try a "Thought-Feeling Diary" which would help you notice when your thoughts are leading to bad feelings. This diary is what it says it is, and you can jot down your thoughts during the day time and see what feelings follow it.

It sounds as if you could really benefit from counseling, maybe a course of CBT (Cognitive Behavioral Therapy). If you can't afford a counselor, you can find lots of information online. This is a tried-and-true method of working on anxiety and depression and would probably greatly benefit you.

How do you deal with a panic attack?

The best way to deal with a panic attack is to ground yourself.

When you feel the panic starting to build and your head begins to swim, grab hold of something like the back of a chair or even lean your back against a wall. Use something to steady yourself because your legs may feel weak.

You will need to use your imagination for the next part of the procedure.

When you are steady and holding on tight bring your attention to the soles of your feet. If you are standing on the ground or if you are seated, feel the carpet or the tiles beneath your feet. Is it a soft or hard surface? How do your feet feel?

Then bring your attention to your hands. Perhaps you are gripping the chair very tightly or pushing against a wall. Feel the tension in your hands, clench them, then unclench them. Then let your fingers relax.

Feel the air on your face. Is it cool or is it warm? Look ahead and focus on one thing in the room. Put all your concentration on that one thing. Look at the color and the shape and see if you can blot out everything else in the room. Just put all your concentration on the thing you are looking at.

Take three deep breaths. Feel the air going in through your nose and out through your mouth. Feel your chest rise and fall.

Now you should be calm and able to let go of the panic. You will feel it subside. Shrug your shoulders, breathe in and breathe out. Sit down and rest for a moment. You will start to feel better now.

How do you remain calm under pressure when somebody is making you anxious and angry?

Nobody can make you be anything you don't want to be. Nobody can make you anxious or even angry. It is up to you to stop allowing them to have power over you.

That's hard to take, isn't it? But it is the only way to remain calm and controlled even in the worst of situations.

Now, examine your relationship with this person and see if it is possible to walk away from the situation. If you are able to just leave the scene there will be no anxiety or anger involved. You just go. That may cause them to become even more angry, but let them be. If you are not there, their anger cannot affect you.

If it is not possible to leave the situation then you must practice being calm while this furor is going on. Shaking with anxiety and shouting in anger take up a great deal of energy, and you give all your power to the other person. And where does it get you in the end? It certainly doesn't stop the argument, and it leaves you feeling totally depleted.

If you look at yourself in your mind's eye, as an observer might, you can imagine sparks of energy emanating from your body, spitting in all directions. See how much energy you are using up. You can only become depleted and succumb to the other person's angry mood if you let it happen.

The best way to cope with this situation is to slow down and reign in your energy level making yourself feel calm. Take long, deep breaths one after the other. Feel your chest rise and fall.

At first, your mind will be racing and you will still want to spit fire at the enemy, but the deeper your breathing becomes the better off you will be. Be still. Be calm. Just stand there and not participate in the argument. Let their words pass through you like smoke.

When you are calm, you can say something like. 'I am not going to argue with you about this'. Nobody can make you argue with them.

What is the difference between panic attack symptoms and heart attack symptoms?

There really isn't any difference when it comes to symptoms that you can observe in yourself.

Panic attack and heart attack can both present with chest/back/jaw pain, nausea, vomiting, sweating, heart palpitations and various other symptoms. When you are experiencing this, it is very difficult to tell whether you are in fact having a heart attack or a panic attack. Both are terrible, but a heart attack is a medical emergency. Panic, though terrifying, is only temporary and doesn't do any long-term damage to the physical body.

The only difference is in the signs. These are clinical results which can be measured if you have a heart attack.

When you arrive at the ER, you will be given an EKG which will show any heart abnormality. If there is a suspicion of a heart attack, you will be given a troponin blood test to measure the level of proteins in your blood. If it is higher than normal levels, it can be interpreted that you have had, or are having, a heart attack. This blood test is often repeated to detect further damage to the heart muscle.

I have been treated for panic attack twice in hospital when I thought I was having a heart attack. It is very frightening, and the symptoms of panic attack make you think you are either going to die or go mad.

I was very embarrassed to find that I had a panic attack, but the doctor assured me that only 20% of the incidence of chest pain relates to the heart. The rest can be indigestion, heart burn or many other minor things. Although panic is not minor, it is better than an actual heart attack.

Do you ever find you create your own anxiety?

I think we always create our own anxiety. It is our anxiety, after all, nobody else's. And we human beings are very creative.

If we are to beat this thing we must think about anxiety and what it is. As human beings we are not naturally anxious about life, but some people live in the future more than others, so they have more anxiety.

If we live in the past, which many people do, there is no anxiety because the past has already happened and there is nothing we can do to change it. We may feel happy, or even sad about the past, but it is over. We may have regrets, but will hopefully learn by our mistakes.

I call anxiety the 'What IF?' disease.

It is based on fear:

- "What if that person doesn't like me?"
- "What if I don't get that raise?"
- "What if I fail my exams?"
- "What if I can't afford the electric bill?"
- "What if I never meet Mr. Right?"

Sometimes we don't even know what we are afraid of but have anxiety most of the time (GAD - General Anxiety Disorder). Some people are anxious about meeting people (Social Anxiety). And others may wash their hands twenty times a day for fear they might catch germs (OCD - Obsessive Compulsive Disorder).

There are many different anxiety disorders, and they are all based on fear of what might happen in the future. Quite often it doesn't even happen, but that doesn't stop us from worrying that it might. It can be very debilitating.

The only way to stop all this anxiety is to get out of the future. Stop thinking about "What If............" and start living in the present.

Living in the past or future is very easy, but living in the present is not. This is because our minds are always working overtime bugging us about everything, and making us feel inadequate. If a person feels inadequate, they will have a lot of anxiety.

But how do we live in the present? Well, we can practice Mindfulness and be conscious of what is going on right here, right now. There is a lot of information about Mindfulness online.

If you are eating an apple, don't eat it aimlessly while worrying about what you should say to your annoying colleague at work, really concentrate on eating that apple. You might like to think about the wonderful smell it has and the crunch it makes between your teeth. Think about the beauty of its form and color. It will make you really appreciate your apple.

The same goes for any other type of activity. If you are washing the dishes, don't start thinking about problems with the kids, think about the smoothness of the dishes and the soapy bubbles that are running through your fingers. If you have a nice smelling washing up liquid, you can breathe that scent in, too.

As you can see this is very hard to do, but if you want to cure your anxiety and quit living in the future it is a good practice.

What do Buddhist monks do?

Chop wood - Carry water.

I don't have any present worries, but I am worried about the future. What can I do to stop this?

People who make long term goals are very often disappointed when they don't come to fruition. Life is totally unpredictable. We cannot know what is in store for us in the future.

How many people marry thinking that they will stay together until either one of them dies? And how many are disappointed when they are signing their divorce papers a few years later? It is a fact that 50% of marriages fail, yet it is so temping to think that yours can work.

How many people have a chosen career path mapped out before them? Their parents may have dictated their career for them, and it is just a matter of following the same route as your mother or father took. Or you may land yourself a really great job and can see yourself climbing to the top of that company. Even being a CEO.

Then, what happens? You find you don't like your job, you are made redundant, you have a family emergency, you get very sick, or you even get run over by a bus. Life can be so disappointing.

I wonder why you should worry about the future at all if you are so happy at this point in your life. Why not make some loose plans and live for today? Life is not meant to be a grueling trial. We are here to be happy and make life happy for other people.

Relax, enjoy the smell of the roses.

I am a very confident person, but I am anxious my partner will judge me negatively. Is there something wrong with me?

You say you are a very confident person, but apparently that is only outside of your relationship. The reason is probably that you are afraid of intimacy. Many people are afraid of intimacy because it makes them feel very vulnerable and afraid their feelings might be hurt. It is as if their feelings are lying on top of their skin, and it is easy to touch them and cause pain.

This is quite natural for a lot of people because we are all afraid of being judged negatively. I don't know whether your partner judges you negatively in all parts of your relationship or not, but what I do know is that, even though you say you are confident, you judge yourself negatively all the time.

It is a fact that when you expect judgement from others it is because you judge yourself mercilessly all the time. The more afraid you are of other people's judgements, the more you judge yourself. You may not realize this because it is something you always do, but to be rid of the fear of judgement you need to stop judging yourself.

That is a tall order, I know. The Judge is something most of us live with quite unknowingly. He is like an unwanted guest who has overstayed his welcome at the party. It is time for him to go and leave you alone to enjoy an intimate relationship.

There is a way to get rid of this unwanted guest, but it is not easy because it is not natural to even notice his presence in your life. The best way to get rid of the Judge is to 'stalk' him. This means you need to be on the lookout for when he pops up again in your life.

Look out for all the times when you tell yourself how stupid, fat, or ugly you are. Look out for the times you go to do something and fear you will mess it up. The Judge is very prominent in your life at these times so it is easier to catch him in the act.

The Judge will be really active when you are trying to be intimate with your partner, so it will be easier to stalk him there. When you are alone with your partner, just acknowledge him and thank him for turning up, but tell him you are not interested in anything he has to say.

You will need to practice this many times over before the Judge will get the message and move on. Finally, when you become aware of the Judge you will be able to laugh at him and send him packing.

How do I beat social anxiety?

Social anxiety is the fear of meeting other people, and it is caused by judgement. When you are afraid to talk, or even be with other people, it is because you are afraid of being judged. It doesn't matter what you are wearing, you always think people are judging you. No matter what comes out of your mouth, you think your words will be judged as well.

If you think about what other people were wearing when you last saw them, you will probably not remember any details, and if you were to try and think what they said you would almost certainly come up short. This is because you are thinking about yourself and the way you are presenting yourself to other people.

People do not concern themselves with what other people are wearing or what they are saying - they are far too busy wondering what other people think of them. Yes, we all do it, some more than others.

There is a simple way out of this dilemma, but like anything else it takes a lot of practice. The answer to social anxiety is to totally take yourself out of the picture. When you enter a room full of other people, see if you can stop thinking about yourself, what you are wearing and what you are saying, and concentrate on the people around you.

When you have your mind off yourself, you can start finding other people so interesting that you completely forget about what you are wearing or what you are saying. It becomes irrelevant.

Keep your focus on other people. The best way to do this is to ask questions. People just love to talk about themselves and will do so nonstop if you allow them. Think about the kind of questions you might ask somebody if you really wanted to get to know them. Practice them in your head, then the next time you are faced with a gathering of people, forget about the impression you are making and ask them questions instead.

Remember to ask open-ended questions, not those that can be answered with a 'yes' or a 'no'. Try not to ask intimate questions, just ask general questions about where they come from or what work they do. Some people can talk about that for hours and, in the end, you can't wait to find somebody else to talk to. Practice this, and very soon you will lose your social anxiety altogether.

Why do some people have a nervous breakdown?

There is no such thing as a nervous breakdown, at least it is not a medical term. People who have 'nervous breakdowns' are those who have been living with more stress than they can handle. They have been working long hours, up all night, not eating properly and generally over-doing it. Something has to give, so they break down.

It is awful, but not a mental illness. It is not like depression as you can usually recover quite quickly from a breakdown, whereas depression often takes weeks or months to recover from. It is certainly not something you want to wish on yourself, though.

If you find yourself having to work long hours, for example, it would be wise to ensure you get enough sleep. It is not enough to party every night, then wonder why you feel so bad the next day. You will need to be disciplined and leave early so that you can get some good quality sleep. Sleep hygiene is often under-stated, but sleep is very important as it is at night that the body rests. If you sleep well, you will be better able to handle your life.

It is also important to eat a proper diet. The body needs fuel, and it cannot live well on junk food or an unbalanced diet. If you are in any doubt about what to eat to stay well, please study which foods are important for good health and which ones are not.

If you are 'burning the candle at both ends' it is important to make time to relax. Study some relaxation exercises and do some creative visualization. Even snatching ten minutes here and there to do some breathing exercises will help to keep you well. There is much information online and it will help you enormously. If you would like to meditate, that can be even better.

Obviously, it is better if you can think of ways to cut back on responsibilities. They have found, scientifically, that people who multitask are not efficient at all. It is far better to concentrate on one thing at a time.

Am I worthy of therapy? I have social anxiety and depression, but have never suffered any kind of abuse because I come from a good family.

I don't really understand what you mean by worthy. You don't need a medical or mental diagnosis to go to therapy. It is a personal choice. If you think it can benefit you, then by all means go and see a good therapist - it often does you good just to talk to someone who will listen.

However, something in your question gives me reason to pause. Why would you question whether you are worthy of therapy? And why can't you decide that for yourself, instead of having to ask a whole world full of strangers on Quora for approval? Why would this person be worthy of therapy, and that person not be worthy of therapy? I think all those things are something to think about.

If you feel worthy as a person, then naturally you are worthy of all the good things in life. I just can't help wondering why you would not feel like a worthwhile person who always needs to seek approval for everything. Even something as worthwhile as therapy.

You say you haven't suffered from any kind of abuse, and come from a good family, so I wonder why you would question your worth? Perhaps you feel that you are worthless as a person. Who has made you feel that way? That can be very debilitating indeed and would cause the social anxiety and depression you speak of.

It sounds as if you have been made to feel ashamed of yourself in the past. Shame is a very damaging emotion, and can ruin a person's life. This could easily amount to abuse. Shame has nothing to do with guilt, they are two very different things. You need to have done something bad to feel guilty. You don't need to have done anything bad to feel shame. Guilt involves an action, but shame is much deeper than that. Shame means you feel bad as a person, a human being.

I felt shame for many, many years, and really hated that commercial on TV that says, '....... because you're worth it'. That used to annoy the hell out of me. Somehow or other, I felt that she was worth having nice shiny hair, and so were all the other people in the world, but I was not. Now, after many years of therapy, I no longer feel all that shame and I can listen to that commercial without feeling a knot in my stomach.

In any case, Quora is not the place to delve deeply into your particular circumstances, but it does sound as if you could really benefit from a course of psychotherapy. Try talk therapy, that will give you some perspective on your problems, and a place to start to repair them.

Good luck.

What is existential anxiety and how can it be managed?

Existential angst is a term used by existentialists to describe the dread a person might feel when talking or thinking about their freedom and responsibilities.

A person generally desires freedom in some form or another, and yet in this life we are rarely free of responsibilities. Even coping day to day involves giving up our freedom with regard to our responsibilities to our family and our work. Some people yearn for freedom their whole lives and can be very disappointed when it does not occur. This can cause a great deal of anxiety.

When talking about the everyday person, the term angst refers to the feeling of deep anxiety they experience when thinking about their own existence here on earth, and the thought of what will happen to them after their death. This is a negative feeling because there are no real answers available. Nobody knows why we are here on earth, and nobody has ever come back to tell us what it is like on the other side. There are no rules, and nobody hands out a Life Manual when you come into this world.

Existentialism has a lot to do with existence as a sentient being. If we exist, then we must spend our time doing something. This is where having a purpose in life is so important. Many people want to know what their purpose is, but they often cannot come up with an answer.

We are always being told we should have a passion, but for most people this is not possible. Most of the time they have no idea what their passion should be. They go to their place of work every day in order to earn money, not from the love of their work. In fact, loving one's job is a luxury in today's society. A few people are fortunate enough to pursue their passion, often in the arts or in non-profit associations, but they generally have to sacrifice some of their freedom due to their responsibilities.

Other people have a deep desire to travel and see other parts of the world. They may even volunteer to work in other countries, but they have to give up a lot of their home comforts in order to experience this freedom.

Then the other side of existentialism becomes important. If we have existence then what are our responsibilities with regard to fulfilling our desires? Are we supposed to develop a life time of learning, or spend our time wisely on other things? Again, there are no rules. This situation of being a sentient being in limbo is very hard for some people to accept and this is where dread and anxiety exist together.

Philosophers have debated this issue for centuries, but like many other things, they have come up with no answers. It is no use saying not to worry about it, I know. But there is not much else we can do.

How do you deal with anxiety without therapy?

You do not necessarily need to go to a therapist for anxiety as you can take medication, or you can work on it yourself.

Anxiety is caused by fear. Usually fear of the future and what might happen if you are not in control. Quite often anxiety occurs about things that never happen, but nonetheless, the fear is there. A lot of people waste time thinking about things that never come to fruition.

If your anxiety is caused by something specific you could work on it at home. Identify exactly what you fear the most then work on that in small increments. If you are afraid of spiders, for example, buy a book on spiders and flash a picture in front of your eyes for less than a second. Then later flash it for a second, then two seconds, then look at the spider which is only a photograph on a page after all and is not going to harm you. Be sure to study it. What color is it? How many legs does it have? Which way do they point? Where are the eyes, etc.?

Then draw a spider of your own. You can make it as elaborate as you like, or even alter and embellish it to your taste. Take your time and make a really beautiful spider.

Then, having done all this, you will realize that you are no longer afraid of spiders, and the chances of you seeing one are not very great either.

Do this with any fear you might have – in small increments - unless you have GAD General Anxiety Disorder where you worry about everything. Then it is time to see a doctor for medication.

What can you do to relax when you have anxiety about an upcoming doctor's appointment?

I am so sorry to hear you are suffering from anxiety about this upcoming appointment, but can understand it as going to see a doctor can be scary for anybody. This is usually the case if you don't go very often, then everything is new to you. And being in a doctor's office can make you feel powerless.

A doctor is an authority figure to many people and they are afraid to speak up and tell the doctor what is wrong. But you have to remember that he/she is there to help you and to give you the benefit of their knowledge. They are not there to intimidate you.

The thing to do is to prepare for the appointment before you go. This means jotting down all the questions you need to ask the doctor. If you don't write them down, chances are you will forget to ask them or you will forget what the doctor has told you. So, go armed with your questions and write down the answers before you leave the surgery. If you are unsure of something, be sure to clarify it while you are there.

Also, learn how to relax so that when you are in the doctor's office you will be better able to cope. Learn some relaxation techniques and apply them in the doctor's office while you are sitting there in front of him. It is a good idea to take a few deep breaths while you are listening to what the doctor has to say, then speak slowly and clearly when it is your time to talk.

Be sure that you understand what he has said and don't be afraid to question anything you are unsure of. It is no use going home and realizing that you didn't understand what he meant about something. It is always wise to ask about it while you are there.

The same goes for medication. Ask about the side effects and weigh up the pros and cons of taking any medication before the doctor writes out the prescription. If you are unsure about which medication you should take, ask his opinion. Always look up your medicines on line when you get home, too, as you want to make informed choices about any treatment you are given for your illness.

Are drama lessons good for coping with anxiety?

Anxiety is based on fear.

Seeing as the worst fear is said to be public speaking, I should think acting in a play would be very difficult if you have anxiety when around other people. It would certainly be a way of conquering that fear, though. Having everybody looking at you, being the literal center of attention, is often an anxious person's nightmare, especially if they suffer from social anxiety where they can barely say, "Boo" to anybody in a public setting. The worst thing would be to force this on anybody. That would probably be a disaster and may well end up in a panic attack.

I used to suffer a lot from anxiety but I like to push myself through it to overcome it. Not everybody's cup of tea. I have tested myself by traveling alone to many places: Frankfurt, Malta, London, Australia three times, and Costa Rica. Also, some short trips to Florida and Seattle. It was a really big test on my nerves but I found that when I was traveling there were so many things to think about that I forgot all about being anxious.

By the time you have sorted out your luggage, gone through the metal detectors, had your luggage searched, waited at stop-overs, watched the boards for flight details, found the right gate – you can be worn out. But overall, I think it did a great deal for my self-confidence and helped enormously with my anxiety.

Traveling alone is really stepping out of your comfort zone and not for everybody. The thing to do is to make sure you have somebody to meet you at the other end. My traveling days are over now. I no longer yearn to see foreign places and am happy at home in Texas.

I really don't know much about acting so you will have to break it down into small pieces like I did with traveling. If you think you can do it, good for you, go for it.

IN CONCLUSION

I hope you have enjoyed reading this book and learned something new from it. It has been a pleasure writing for you.

Bipolar is a difficult illness to handle at the best of times, but when things go wrong, they can be devastating. If you have found something useful in this book, I hope you will put it into practice.

Remember, when it comes to bipolar there is always hope.

Hope is what keeps us keeping on.

All the very best to you,

Sally Alter

https://wirsinddu.eu/sally_alter

If you think this book would be of help to others, please consider leaving a review on Amazon.

BIOGRAPHY

Sally Alter. Photo Credit: Randie Benno

Sally Alter was born in London and has spent her life traveling around the world. She is an R.N. (Registered Nurse) who has lived with bipolar 1 for over 50 years. Her answers to over 800 questions on bipolar and mental health have been viewed 13 million times on Quora to date. She has overcome enormous hardships in her life and is passionate about helping others to enjoy life with bipolar.

Sally now lives in Texas with her writing, her artwork and her two cats Greta and Tiger.

TESTIMONIALS

" HOW TO LIVE WITH BIPOLAR" has given me tremendous insight and appreciation for those who face bipolar issues daily. Sally Alter answers questions and offers advice based on her own experience living with bipolar. I highly recommend her book to anyone searching for information and reassurance for themselves or a loved one."
Kathleen Pennell, M.Ed. Author of 13 books.

" Sally Alter really hit the mark with this unique book. She has life experience and knowledge, and has generously shared it with others here."
Randie Benno, Mental Health Peer Support Specialist.

" HOW TO LIVE WITH BIPOLAR is the superlative read one would expect from the most viewed Quora bipolar author. With an astounding 13 million content views, 3,000 + answered questions and nearly 6,000 followers, Sally Alter brings the same level of knowledge, candor, wit, and wisdom to these 125 questions. User-friendly and informative, the world needs this book. Bottom line: Anyone who purchases this book will also be sold on it. Guaranteed."
David A. Feingold, D.Ed. Author of Stigma.

" Sally Alter's book is a heartfelt and experiential description of bipolar disorder. I believe it will be extremely helpful for those struggling with this terrible illness, or friends and family members who need to understand what it is like to suffer with bipolar disorder. I feel this book would also be helpful for those interested in psychology and researching bipolar disorder."
Jon Shore, Psychotherapist, specializing in depression and anxiety disorders.

" An incredibly honest, insightful look at the ways in which bipolar disorder affects every area of your life. Sally gives a fantastic blend of medical advice and personal experience that feels as though she is right there beside you, hopeful and encouraging, shining the light towards the end of the tunnel. It will keep you reading all night!"
Michele Abbott, B.Sc. Quora writer.

" This book has an unbelievable amount of information, and is written from such a personal perspective that I am sure it will help lots of people that suffer with this horrible illness."
Carmen Forrest, founder of Wirsinddu.eu.

Printed in Great Britain
by Amazon